African Primal Religions

Major World Religions Series

Donald K. Swearer, Editor

African
Primal Religions

BY ROBERT CAMERON MITCHELL, Ph.D

Argus Communications
A Division of DLM, Inc.
Niles, Illinois U.S.A.

ACKNOWLEDGEMENTS

Excerpt from *Ifa Divination: Communication Between Gods and Men in West Africa* by William Bascom, copyright © 1969 by Indiana University Press. Reprinted by permission of the publisher.

Excerpt from *African Traditional Religion: A Definition* by E. B. Idowu. Copyright © SCM Press Ltd., 1973. U.S. Edition Orbis Books, Maryknoll, N.Y. 10545.

Excerpts from *Olodumare: God in Yoruba Belief* by E. B. Idowu. Copyright © 1966 by Longman Group Ltd., Harlow, Essex, England. Reprinted by permission of the publisher.

Excerpts from Gunter Wagner, "The Abaluyia of Kavirondo (Kenya)" in Daryll Forde, ed., *African Worlds*. Copyright © 1954 by International African Institute, London, and Gunter Wagner. Reprinted by permission of the International African Institute and Mrs. Gunter Wagner.

PHOTO CREDITS

John Collier   84B
Jane P. Downton/TOM STACK & ASSOCIATES   cover: right
Bill N. Kleeman/TOM STACK & ASSOCIATES   cover: top center; 16
Lloyd A. McCarthy/TOM STACK & ASSOCIATES   cover: left
Robert Cameron Mitchell   cover: center; 9, 29, 41, 56, 84T, 92
Barbara von Hoffman/TOM STACK & ASSOCIATES   cover: bottom

MAPS

Homer Grooman

COVER DESIGN

Gene Tarpey

Printed in the United States of America.

Argus Communications
A Division of DLM, Inc.
7440 Natchez Avenue
Niles, Illinois 60648 U.S.A.

International Standard Book Number: 0-913592-97-8

Library of Congress Number: 77-82795

0 9 8 7 6 5 4

For Douglas, Timothy, and Stuart

Contents

Foreword

"The study of religion is the study of mankind." Religion touches the deepest feelings of the human heart and is part of every human society. In modern times religion has been studied by sociologists and anthropologists as a cultural institution. Psychologists see religion as an expression of an inner human need. Philosophers view it as a system of thought or doctrine. Historians consider religion a part of the intellectual and institutional development of a given era.

What is religion? Modern definitions range from "what man does in his solitude" to "an expression of collective identity," and from "man's experience of awe and fascination before a tremendous mystery" to "projective feelings of dependency." The scope of life that religion is identified with is so vast, and the assumptions about the nature of religion are so varied, that we may readily agree with those who say that the study of religion is the study of mankind.

Religion takes many forms, or perhaps it would be better to say that there are many aspects to religion. They include *belief* (e.g., the belief in a creator God), *ritual action* (e.g., making offerings to that God), *ethical action* (following God's law), the formation of *religious communities,* and the formulation of *creeds and doctrinal systems.*

Joachim Wach, a scholar of religion, has pictured religion in terms of religious experience which expresses itself in thought, action, and fellowship.[1] In this view religion is rooted in religious experience, and all other aspects of religion are expressions of that experience. For example, the Buddha's experience of the highest Truth (in Buddhism called *Nirvana*) led him to teach what he had experienced (known as *dharma*) and resulted in the formation of a monastic community (known as *sangha*).

It must be remembered that religions develop within particular historical and cultural traditions and not in a vacuum. This fact has several profound consequences for the study of religion. In the first place it means that religion can never be completely separated from particular historical and cultural traditions. For example, early Christian thought was deeply influenced by both Semitic and Greek

---

[1]Joachim Wach, *The Comparative Study of Religions* (New York: Columbia University Press, 1958).

traditions, and such central Christian celebrations as Christmas and Easter owe their form to pre-Christian European traditions.

Furthermore, since a religion is subject to cultural and historical influences, its traditions are always developing relative to particular times and places. For example, the form of worship used in the Buddhist Churches of America (founded in the late nineteenth century) has as much or more in common with American Protestant worship services than with its traditional Japanese form. A religion, then, as part of a specific historical and cultural stream, changes through time and can be fully understood only in relationship to its historical and cultural forms. By way of generalization we might say that Christianity as a religion is only partially understood in terms of its central beliefs and that a fuller or more complete understanding demands a knowledge of its worldwide history and the influence of its various cultural traditions.

In the second place, since a religion develops within particular historical and cultural settings, it also influences its setting. In other words, there is a give-and-take relationship between a religion and its environment. For example, in traditional societies like medieval Europe, Christianity was the inspiration for much of the art and architecture. The same is true for traditional India, where Buddhism and Hinduism decisively affected artistic forms, or for traditional Persia with Islam. Of course, religion influences its environment in other than merely artistic realms. It has had profound effects on modes of behavior (ethics), conceptions of state (politics), forms of economic endeavor—indeed, on all aspects of life.

As a consequence of the pervasive influence of religion in so many aspects of human endeavor, students of religion and society have observed that in traditional societies religion was never isolated. That is, nothing within the given society was perceived as nonreligious or profane. Every meaningful act was seen as religious or sacred. Professor Robert Bellah of the University of California at Berkeley argues that in the West the split between the sacred and the profane or the differentiation of religion from other aspects of life did not really begin until about the time of the Protestant Reformation. He refers to that period as "early modern." Beginning with the early modern period onward to the present, religion has become more and more differentiated from Western culture. Thus, for example, it is no longer assumed that an American is a Protestant, whereas it is still largely assumed that a Thai is a Buddhist.

The question has been asked, "Can someone understand a religion in which he or she does not believe?" As the previous discussion of the nature of religion indicates, belief in the truth claims of a religious tradition is not a prerequisite for engaging in its study or even for understanding (i.e., making sense of) its beliefs and historical forms. The study of religion, however, does demand empathy and sympathy. To engage in the study of another religion for the purpose of proving that one's own is superior can only result in a distorted understanding of that tradition. Or, for that matter, if one who professes no religious belief approaches the study of religion with an inhibiting skepticism, then the beauty and richness of religion will be lost. For the believer, the study of another religious tradition should enhance his or her own faith-understanding; for the nonbeliever (i.e., agnostic), the study of religion should open up new dimensions of the human spirit.

The objective study of religion should be undertaken because of its inherent significance—because the understanding of cultures and societies, indeed, of humankind, is severely limited when such study is ignored. The study of our own tradition from its own particular creedal or denominational perspective is justifiably a part of our profession of faith. However, such study should not close us off from a sympathetic understanding of other religious traditions. Rather, such inquiry should open us to what we share in common with other religious persons, as well as to what is genuinely unique about our own religious beliefs and traditions.

Is the study of religion relevant today? The authors of this series believe the answer is a resounding "Yes!" The United States—indeed, the world—is in the midst of a profound transition period. The crisis confronting nations today cannot be reduced merely to economic inflation, political instability, and social upheaval. It is also one of values and convictions. The time has passed when we can ignore our crying need to reexamine such basic questions as who we are and where we are going—as individuals, as communities, and as a nation. The interest in Islam on the part of many American blacks, experimentation with various forms of Asian religions by the "Age of Aquarius" generation, and a resurgence of Christian piety on college campuses are particular responses to the crisis of identity through which we are currently passing.

The serious study of religion in the world today is not only legitimate but necessary. Today we need all of the forces we can muster in order to restore a sense of individual worth, moral community, and value direction. The sympathetic study of religion can contribute toward these goals and can be of assistance in helping us to recover an awareness of our common humanity too long overshadowed by our preoccupation with technological and material achievement. As has been popularly said, we have conquered outer space at the expense of inner space.

But why study non-Western religions? The reason is quite simple. We no longer live in relative isolation from the cultures of Asia and Africa. As a consequence the marketplace of ideas, values, and faiths is much broader than it used to be. We are in contact with them through popular books and the news media, but for the most part our acquaintance is superficial at best. Rather than looking at the religions imbedded in these cultures as quaint or bizarre—an unproductive enterprise—we should seek genuine understanding of them in the expectation of broadening, deepening, and hopefully clarifying our own personal identity and direction. The study of religion is, then, a twofold enterprise: engaging the religion(s) as it is, and engaging ourselves in the light of that religion.

The Argus Communications Major World Religions Series attempts to present the religious traditions of Judaism, Christianity, Islam, Hinduism, Buddhism, China, and Africa in their unity and variety. On the one hand, the authors interpret the traditions about which they are writing as a faith or a world view which instills the lives of their adherents with value, meaning, and direction. On the other hand, each volume attempts to analyze a particular religion in terms of its historical and cultural settings. This latter dimension means that the authors are interested in the present form of a religious tradition as well as its past development. How can Christianity or Judaism speak to the problems confronting Americans today? What are some of the new religions of Africa, and are they displacing traditional beliefs and world views? Can Maoism be considered the new religion of China? Is traditional Hinduism able to cope with India's social, economic, and political change? The answers to such questions form a legitimate and important part of the content of the series.

The author of each volume is a serious student and teacher of the tradition about which he or she is writing. Each has spent considerable time in countries where that religious tradition is part of the culture. Furthermore, as individuals, the authors are committed to the positive value the proper study of religion can have for students in these times of rapid social, political, and economic change. We hope that the series succeeds in its attempt to present the world's religions not as something "out there," a curiosity piece of times past, but as a subject of study relevant to the needs of our times.

Chapter 1

Introduction

In many respects the religions described in this book will be very strange to you. They are the religions of the peoples of Africa who lived, until recently, in societies which were organized at the tribal level of social organization. These tribal societies, like their counterparts all over the world, do not have written languages and very few have cities. Their technology is extremely simple in comparison with that of the Western world, although their culture is rich and complex. Perhaps the most striking difference between traditional African culture and Western culture, however, is the sense of sacredness, of religious mystery, of spiritual powers which pervades every aspect of African traditional life.

Almost one hundred years ago Max Weber, the famous German sociologist, wrote in his book entitled *The Protestant Ethic and the Spirit of Capitalism* that modern life was becoming *demystified*. This was the consequence, he argued, of that relentless pursuit of rationality in all areas of life which had made modern industrial society unique in world history. Modern life was measured, understood, made calculable and predictable in ways that were inconceivable before 1800. The increase in productivity and the resulting affluence were phenomenal. As economic life became established in modern capitalism, as impersonal but efficient bureaucracy developed, as the advances in science began to rapidly expand knowledge of the world, and as technology applied these advances to virtually every area of life, the inevitable consequence was the loss of the sense of mystery and sacredness which had hitherto permeated all human societies in one way or another.

Since Weber's analysis of Western society, the process of demystification has continued unabated. Today even sex and death are studied scientifically! It is not surprising that there has been something of a reaction against this harsh secularization in recent years. Many people today are fascinated by events which seem to fall outside of scientific explanation, such as flying saucers or the dread effect of the Bermuda Triangle on ships and airplanes. Millions of North Americans seek knowledge about their personal futures from the daily horoscope

1

column, despite the recent statement by a group of noted astronomers that astrology is nonsense. Some seek to resolve anxiety and tension through Transcendental Meditation and other forms of meditation. Others seek salvation in one or the other of the various imported religions which offer the ancient wisdom of India, Japan, Africa, and first-century Palestine to modern office workers and professionals.

There is something pathetic about many of these imported religious cults which seek to provide a way to remystify life for their believers. Although such cults claim to be authentic importations of the original version, they are often merely boiled-down versions specifically tailored for busy Canadians or Americans. Some of them are so commercialized that they seem to have as their major purpose the financial enrichment of their leaders. This is a pity, because these religions in the context of their original culture have a wholeness and grace which offer a useful counterpoint to the spiritual aridity of much of modern life.

It is the aim of this book to show you the African primal religions, that is, the traditional religions of black Africa, or Africa as it was prior to contact with the West or with Islam. Much that seems strange about these religions will be understandable when you see how they fit into the way of life of traditional Africans. By putting yourself into tribal culture, through the use of your imagination, you may also gain some understanding of the "world we have lost," where spiritual powers were everyday realities and where humans and nature shared a certain sacredness. You will also see the dark side of this traditional world, because ignorance and fear of evil powers are an inescapable part of these religions. Finally, you will gain an understanding of modern Africa as well, because much of the assumptions in the traditional African world view continue to be the assumptions that influence the lives of many African Christians and Muslims.

BLACK AFRICA

The continent of Africa contains two culturally distinct Africas. The countries north of the great Sahara comprise North Africa and have an Arab Muslim culture. Thus, for the most part, they have more in common with their fellow Arab nations in the Middle East than with their black African neighbors to the south. This book is not concerned with these northern countries. The Africa which it describes, known as black Africa, lies south of the Sahara. Although some of the peoples in this area have been Muslim for centuries, they are African, not Arab, Muslims. With the exception of the peoples who live in Ethiopia, which is unique in other ways as well, and Liberia, most of them live in countries which have recently emerged from about one hundred years of colonial rule. Since 1957 some thirty-eight African nations have gained their independence from France, Britain, Belgium, Portugal, and Spain. Now only the countries near the tip of Africa—Rhodesia, Namibia (South-West Africa), and South Africa—remain to be liberated from white-settler domination.

Black Africa covers a large area and contains more than 200 million people. It is a continent in change. Every government is committed to modernization. Industrial development, mass communication, education, modern medicine, and modern transportation systems are being introduced as fast as the resources of the new nations will permit. Large towns and cities, which were virtually unknown in most of traditional Africa, are commonplace, and some have mushroomed to more than one million inhabitants. Many people are giving up the religion of their ancestors for Islam or Christianity.

Development is a slow and difficult process. Many of these countries are among the world's poorest, with per capita incomes of $100 or less. Today the vast majority of the black African population continue to be farmers. When one drives outside the very modern cities, one finds villages just a few miles away where much of the daily life and customs are the same as they were prior to colonialization. One of the major problems that African leaders face is how to get people to stop thinking of themselves as tribal members, that is, as Yoruba or Ibo or Ashanti or Kikuyu, and to think of themselves instead as Nigerian or Ghanaian or Kenyan.

In the last two chapters of this book we will look at the place that the African primal religions occupy in contemporary Africa. However, *most of this book will focus on traditional Africa.* We need to understand what these primal religions were like before we can see how they are changing and what influence they continue to have in contemporary Africa.

AN INTRODUCTION TO IBADAN
AND THE YORUBA

When I was in college, I remember talking with a friend of mine about his trip to West Africa. Even though he was still a college student, he was also an official in an international student religious group and had recently visited Ghana and Nigeria in the course of his duties. Even as I avidly questioned him about his experiences, the notion of realizing my dream and actually going to Africa myself seemed inconceivable. Black Africa seemed so very far away! This was in 1956 and black Africa was rarely in the news, although this began to change in the next year, 1957, when Ghana became one of the first black African nations to become independent. At that time, very few universities taught courses on Africa. The idea that African history was worth teaching was a controversial one. Many people thought that Africans were savages and did not have any history apart from the history of the English, French, and Portuguese colonizers. In those days even black Americans preferred to ignore their African background. Nevertheless, three years later, in 1960, I found myself in the city of Ibadan, Nigeria, where I was to live for two years teaching and doing research. Twice more I have returned to Ibadan for research, and I have also had the chance to visit almost half of the independent black African nations as well as South Africa.

Ibadan is an amazing city. Its inhabitants are members of the Yoruba tribe (at about ten million people, really a nation), one of the largest of Nigeria's forty or fifty tribes. Today the city is the capital of the western state of Nigeria and has a population of over one million (about the population of Houston, the sixth most populous city in the United States)! Even in 1841, the year when the first white visitor entered the walled city, its population was one hundred thousand. Anthropologists call Yoruba cities "ethnographic anomalies" because tribal peoples usually live in small villages.

Despite the small but growing number of skyscrapers and the middle-class suburban housing developments which are spreading around the outskirts of the old city, the bulk of the houses are still made of the traditional mud wall construction. Crowded very close together, the houses are arranged every which way and sprawl endlessly across the city's hills. Narrow alleyways rub between the houses, occasionally opening onto an incredibly busy marketplace. The whole effect is more similar to medieval London or Paris than to other more modern African cities such as Dakar, Accra, or Nairobi. Only a few modern roads slash their way across the older part of the city, but now the whole city is oriented toward these roads, just as it is oriented toward the developing modern economy of Nigeria, black Africa's most populous country (about 65 million) and also one of its wealthiest.

It has well been said that no place in Africa is typical yet every place is African. We have to start our exploration of African primal religions someplace, and Ibadan is that place and the Yoruba are the people. Try and put aside whatever preconceptions, stereotypes, and prejudices you may have about African religion, therefore, and consider just one aspect of the multifaceted and complex set of rituals and beliefs which make up Yoruba religion—the annual Egungun festival.

THE EGUNGUN FESTIVAL

It is early in June and 'Dele is very excited. Tomorrow the Egungun festival takes place. The rains came early this year in March, and the new yams have been ready to be harvested for a while. 'Dele is anxious to taste the new yams, but he knows that until the Egungun festival occurs they must not be harvested.

'Dele is fourteen now. When he was a young boy, he used to be very frightened by the Egungun masqueraders with their mysterious masked appearance, the weird unnatural voices they used, and their sometimes threatening manner. "It is an Egungun, an ancestor returned," his mother had said to him once, years ago, when they encountered a hideously masked figure near the Oje market leading a small crowd of young men with whips and flanked by five drummers pounding a fierce rhythm. 'Dele watched, trembling, as his mother calmly knelt with some other women and asked the Egungun for a blessing. As 'Dele grew up and learned more about the Egungun, he heard many blessings similar to the one he heard on that day. Here is one of them translated from the Yoruba language:

Whatever your plans, they will succeed.
Ajayi, death will not pass through your house!
Disease will not lay you low!
The one who tries to poison you will poison himself!
The Angel of Death will not wrest your child away from you!
You will never suffer the humiliation of being told "come and
    eat food" like a pet animal!
Your eye will not suffer blindness.
No child of yours will die and vanish from your sight!
Just as a cat's fur lasts till old age and life reaches its span,
    so shall you enjoy luck till you age and pass away.

THE ANCESTORS

For 'Dele it seems natural for the ancestors to come among the living. His father has already told him some of the myths of the Yoruba which he had learned from his father before him. Through these stories, which explain the Yoruba way of life and its meaning, 'Dele knows that a person's spirit exists before birth and continues after death. The ancestral spirits have the potential power to affect the living both for good, if they are respectfully and properly venerated, and for evil, if their worship is neglected. His father regularly pours libations, or liquids such as palm wine, as an offering to his ancestors before eating a meal. Once a year special sacrifices are made in a corner

5

of the compound over 'Dele's grandfather's grave. And he now knows that the men of his family inherit membership in the Egungun Society.

All Yoruba venerate the ancestors, of course, but the Egungun is a secret men's society which is particularly concerned with the ancestors, just as the members of the Oro Society are especially concerned with fighting witchcraft. His father meets with the other members periodically in the Egungun grove over toward Offa Hill, and soon 'Dele will become a member of the society and go with his father to those meetings.

ORDER AND BALANCE

Already 'Dele knows much about the Egungun Society but not their deep secrets. Like every person, he knows that the masquerade costumes are worn by men such as his uncle, Folorunsho, who will wear the dreaded costume of Ololu on the last day of the festival. But although everybody knows that it is a man under the costume, women must never see the face or the body of the masquerader, even if his costume should accidentally rip. In the old days, women were killed under such circumstances.

This does not happen in modern Nigeria, of course, but 'Dele is enough of a traditionalist to understand why death was the necessary penalty. For women to see the man under the mask is to break a taboo. It is to violate deeply the sacred order of the world. The balance in the relationship between men and the gods and between men and women has become disturbed and must be righted. In like manner, no one should touch the dress of an Egungun in public because it is believed that the costumes are charged with ancestral power. As the proverb says, "Even a prince cannot go near an Egungun without suffering the consequences." What seems ordinary and everyday, like cloth, drums, and even his uncle, for a time takes on an extraordinary dimension. His uncle will become possessed; at the height of the festival he will be so filled with the ancestor Ololu that he will literally not be himself.

That night the family keeps the vigil, kneeling and praying to invoke the blessings and aid of the departed parents. A goat is killed and its blood poured on the graves of the ancestors as a sacrifice. Early in the morning the excitement builds. The first day of the festival has come. 'Dele's father goes off to the grove where the Egungun are preparing their costumes. As 'Dele hurries to the king's compound (a set of houses inside an enclosure), he passes thousands of people who are out on the streets. All of them seem to be in a very festive mood.

THE EGUNGUN

The day has grown very hot by the time 'Dele presses his way into the courtyard of the king's compound. He tries to keep out of the way of the young men who arrogantly push the crowd around to keep the center of the compound open for the Egungun. At last the distant drums grow louder, the crowd stirs, and suddenly the Egungun enter. There is Alapanshipa; here are Atipako and Labala! Over there are many others. Each has a unique costume made up of many multi-colored strips of cloth, with red as the dominant color. Some are covered with powerful charms. Some wear wooden masks while the heads of others are simply covered with a transparent or webbed cloth. Like Yoruba society, with its kings and chiefs, there is a status hierarchy of the Egungun, the lesser Egungun giving way before the major ones. Indeed some masqueraders, known as olotiki, are simply entertainers who perform amazing acrobatics.

SOME MYTHS

'Dele knows why red is a dominant color of the Egungun. His father has told him that it is the color of the goddess Oya. According to the myth, Oya comes from Nupe, a country to the north. She is the patroness of the Egungun because Egungun was her son.

> Oya was the wife of Ogun (the god of iron) and could not have children. She consulted a diviner who revealed that she could have sons with a man who possessed her violently. Shango (the god of thunder) took her. Oya had nine sons by him. The first eight were born dumb. Again . . . Oya consulted the diviner who told her to make sacrifices. The result was the birth of Egungun or Egun, who was not dumb but could only speak with a voice which was not human.[1]

'Dele remembers another myth his uncle once told him which explains why people believe that the Egungun cloths have such power.

> Once there was an epidemic. We are not certain what it was, we only know what the god of divination says it was—a dread illness that killed thousands, leaving deadly little spots broken out on people's bodies. Diviners said to carry three red cloths, called eku, to a certain spot and sacrifice there to save the city. At this place the carriers of the cloth met the spirits of the disease. The latter fled at the sight of the three red cloths.[2]

THE KING'S BLESSING

Youths wielding whips precede the Egungun and clear the way. For what seems a long time to 'Dele, there is a constant movement back and forth in the compound. Some Egungun dance on one spot to the special intricate rhythms of their drummers. Others suddenly burst forward in one direction, the drummers hastily backing away before them but still drumming and facing the dancers. The dancing and the drumming articulate in a complex and, to 'Dele, inspiring interplay. At last the Egungun go forward to receive the king's blessing. The king says solemnly:

Eku odan	Salute for the feast
Opo re ni eshe	Abundance in what you do
Olorun yio ma so yin	God will speak to you
Kekerere l'Olorun gbe yin	God has established you
kale	from your early years[3]

'Dele is caught up in the excitement and feels at the same time both fear and love for the ancestors.

A Yoruba Egungun masquerader in an Ibadan neighborhood.

SACRED DANGER

Then with a tremendous drumming and tumult the Egungun go forth from the king's compound to dance around the town for the next week. Throughout the city people pay their respects to the ancestors through the Egungun. Even elderly people kneel before the masqueraders to pay their homage. It is a time of gaiety and high energy, of buffoonery and frolic, yet it is tinged with potential violence, like the carnival in Rio de Janeiro or the running of the bulls in Pamplona, Spain. It is also the time when the new yams are brought by the chiefs and put in the four corners of the town and on the shrines of the Egungun and the many other gods or divinities that the Ibadan people worship. Corn pap and bean cake are also put on the Egungun shrines. The ancestors being satisfied, the living can now partake in the first harvest with confidence. Sacrifices are made, through the Egungun, by the children of parents who have died during the course of the year.

For 'Dele as for most people, the climax of the festival comes when Ololu makes his appearance at the end of the week. At this time the circuslike mood recedes and the atmosphere becomes especially charged. The markets are closed. Ololu is known as an Egungun ogun, a war Egungun, as he was captured from one of Ibadan's Yoruba enemies in a war fought long ago. His ancestral power has a special potency and danger, perhaps because his foreign origin makes him more inclined to punish breaches of the moral order without favoritism. Following Ololu's appearance, the ancestors recede and disappear from view for the time being. Egungun will appear from time to time at funerals and other occasions during the year, and of course the ancestors are always watching the living; but their full presence will not be felt communally by the city until the rains and the growth of the yams signal the time for the next Egungun festival.

African primal religions do not have founders like Jesus or the Buddha, or sacred scriptures like the Holy Bible or the Koran. Therefore, immersion in a *single* celebration like the Egungun festival and its various meanings is the best way to begin to understand these religions. At this point, however, we need to take a larger view and consider these religions as a whole. What are African primal religions? How do they fit into traditional African culture? Why are they worth studying? How have they been affected by the modernization of Africa? How do they differ from religions in North America, like Christianity and Judaism?

We will begin our search for the answers to these questions in the next chapter, which considers an important paradox and basic truth about the African primal religions: These religions are many but one.

Chapter 2

Many But One

The title of this book is *African Primal Religions,* not *African Primal Religion.* The addition of that *s* is deliberate. One of the important characteristics of African religions is their tribal and local character. In this chapter we will discover that there are as many African primal religions as there are African tribes. We will discover that the world view that lies behind these many religions is one. But first it is necessary to learn something about African tribes, because tribal and village Africa is the setting for African religions. The Africa described here is traditional Africa before the colonization and modernization of the past one hundred years or so. How the primal religions have changed will be discussed at the end of this book.

CONCEPT OF TRIBE

How would you define *tribe?* If you think of a preliterate people who share a common culture or way of life, you have only part of the answer because there are some peoples in Africa who share very similar cultures and languages but who view themselves as separate peoples. The second part of the definition of *tribe,* therefore, is a *shared sense of identity.* The people also have to view themselves as one people—to act on the belief that they are Kipsigis rather than Nandi (two tribes in Kenya) or Ibo rather than Ibibio (two tribes in Nigeria). Because the criteria for dividing the peoples of Africa up into separate tribes involve such a subjective factor, it is sometimes hard to say with definite authority whether a particular people are a separate tribe or merely a subgroup of a larger people. This is made even more difficult by the fact that the sense of belonging together often changes over time as a result of warfare or migrations. Today's tribe may have been yesterday's subgroup or vice versa.

It is therefore difficult to say exactly how many tribes there are in black Africa, but the figure of two thousand is commonly given. The map of Africa (p. 12) shows how George Peter Murdock, the noted

PEOPLES AND
REGIONS OF AFRICA

NORTHERN

WESTERN

Bundyaranke

Mende

Ashanti

H a u s a

Yoruba
IBADAN
Ga   ibo
ini
Ibibio
Kalabari

Tiv

Nuer

EASTERN

Galla

Lugbara

Lup
Baganda   Abaluyia   Kikuyu
Kipsigis
Nandi

CENTRAL   Pygmies

K o n g o

Lele

Lake
Victoria

M a s a i

Bushmen

SOUTHERN

American anthropologist, has charted the location of some tribes.[1] As you can see, traditional Africa is a mosaic of many different independent peoples. Until recently, most of them lived in relative isolation from all but their neighboring peoples. But it is important to point out that traditional African society was not totally static and unchanging by any means. Over the past thousand years, for example, several large kingdoms like Ghana and Mali emerged in West Africa, the Bantu-speaking peoples gradually migrated thousands of miles southward as far as South Africa from present-day eastern Nigeria and the Cameroons, and various peoples were conquered by other peoples and lost their cultural identity as they merged with their conquerors. Finally, some of the coastal peoples, like the Kongo tribe in Angola and Zaire and the Bini tribe in Nigeria, had sustained contact with Portuguese traders as early as the fifteenth century.

TRIBAL COMPARISONS

How do these two thousand tribes compare with each other culturally? This is an important question for us because, as we will see, African primal religions are closely related to African cultures. Despite the fact that all these peoples are at the tribal level of social organization, their ways of life vary quite a bit. An examination of various aspects of African tribes will reveal these differences.

1. *Size.* There is enormous variation in the size of African tribes. Some of the smallest number only a few thousand people while the largest ones, like the Yoruba, Hausa, and Ibo in Nigeria, each include ten million people or so, making them larger than many of the world's nations.

2. *Size of settlement unit.* The Yoruba are unique in having large walled cities as their traditional settlements. Many African peoples live in villages of fifty to three hundred although some, like the Kikuyu, live in homesteads scattered across the countryside.

3. *Political organization.* Some peoples, like the Ashanti of Ghana and the Baganda of Uganda, live in centralized chiefdoms. There the paramount chief rules over subordinate chiefs who rule the people. Others do not have chiefs at all, like the Tiv of Nigeria. Still others have village chiefs as the highest form of political authority.

4. *Descent patterns.* Most African peoples trace their descent back through only the father or the mother. (Anthropologists call this unilineal descent.) Compare this with the United States and Canada where descent is traced and property is inherited through both the mother's and the father's sides of the family. Most often descent is traced through the father's side by Africans (called patrilineal

descent), but about 20 percent of African peoples (including the Ashanti) trace their descent and inherit property through their mother's side (matrilineal descent).

5. *Family patterns.* The traditional African's family is far more "extended" than ours. People we would count as distant relatives, such as second cousins, are typically treated as close relatives by Africans. Furthermore, a relatively large number of relatives often live together in the same house or compound with a married couple and their children. Such an extended family might include grandparents, and uncles and aunts with their children.

6. *Marriage patterns.* Polygamy is permitted by most African tribes, although the percentage of the men in a tribe who actually have more than one wife varies. Thus many African households have not only various relatives living together but also co-wives and their children.

7. *Mode of living.* The most important distinction to be made here is between those Africans who are nomadic cattle herders and those who are settled farmers. About 80 percent of African peoples practice agriculture and live in settled villages. Traditionally, each family would raise just enough crops to provide for its own needs and to trade for a few essentials. The land was owned by the group rather than by individuals. Unlike India and the peasant areas of Latin America, there were no landlords who took rent in traditional Africa and no moneylenders. Because the population density in most parts of Africa was low, if a man needed more land he just asked the family head or the chief for a further allotment. And if a man stopped using certain land which was still fertile, it could be redistributed to someone else who needed it. In contrast, the nomadic cattle herders like the Fulani of West Africa and the Masai and Galla in East Africa have quite a different way of life. It is not surprising that the religion of these peoples centers on cattle while the religion of the agriculturalists focuses on the land and fertility. The nomadic peoples have also been much more resistant to the pressures of modernization than the agricultural peoples. They have been reluctant to give up their way of life and to seek modern schooling for their children.

You may have heard of the Pygmies and the Bushmen. These peoples, who are short in stature, also live in Africa and practice still another and very ancient way of life, that of hunting and gathering. Traditionally, they neither tilled fields nor raised cattle but lived as humanity's ancestors lived before the discovery of agriculture and the domestication of animals some fifteen thousand years ago. The number of Pygmies and Bushmen is very small—in the tens of thousands—and today their way of life is fast disappearing.

8. *Technological level.* Ancient Africans had a relatively simple technology. To be sure they knew how to smelt and work iron and had highly sophisticated techniques for casting bronze statues and working precious metals like gold. Animals were domesticated, and skillful farming techniques were developed. But the wheel was unknown, as was writing. Consequently, communication and transportation were very limited; only trails or sometimes rivers linked communities, as there were no roads and no wheeled vehicles. Without writing, traditions were passed down through an oral process. Instead of written scriptures or history books, therefore, there were specialists with highly trained memories who preserved the tribal traditions down through the generations.

CLOSED COMMUNITIES

Taking into consideration these characteristics of African tribal societies, we can generalize that much of traditional Africa is composed of small-scale, relatively self-contained, and relatively homogeneous communities. This is what distinguishes African tribesmen from peasants. In Asia, southern Europe, and Central and South America, peoples at the present level of social organization live in societies that have cities, a literate culture, a universal religion (Buddhism, Hinduism, Roman Catholicism), landowners, and a large cultural gap between the simple peasant and the urban elite. Only in parts of Ethiopia, where Christianity and literacy have been present for several thousand years, has a true peasantry developed in Africa.

Rural communities in Canada and the United States are more conservative than the cities and suburbs. By comparison, traditional African society is super-rural. People grow up and live and die in the same village among the same people. Until recently, most Africans in times of peace seldom encountered people from faraway villages and only rarely people from other tribes. Therefore, until recently the accustomed way of doing things was the *only* way that people knew. The Yoruba or Ibo or Kikuyu or Ashanti way of life was seen as *the* proper way for a person to live. Alternative ways to act or believe were unknown.

Robin Horton, a British anthropologist, refers to this absence of alternatives when he calls African traditional cultures "closed" cultures.[2] In scientifically oriented cultures, an awareness of alternatives is highly developed, making Western culture, in this sense, an extremely "open" society. Medieval Europe and puritan New England

were somewhere in between. This insight is further developed later in this chapter in the discussion of the oneness of African primal religions.

TRIBAL RELIGIONS

Now we are ready to return to the statement that was made at the beginning of this chapter—that there are as many primal religions as there are tribes. In Africa, religion and the tribal group are inseparable. Religion is simply a part of the tribal culture, of the tribal way of life, and practicing the religion is a totally taken-for-granted requirement of living in that culture. Until the recent changes brought about by modernization and colonialism, being a Yoruba necessarily involved believing in the Yoruba gods and participating in the rituals of Yoruba religion, just as being a member of the Kikuyu tribe in Kenya involved participating in Kikuyu rituals and worshipping the Kikuyu gods. The idea of a Yoruba trying to convert a Kikuyu to his or her religion is unthinkable because it would be the same thing as asking the Kikuyu to become a Yoruba.

Compare the plurality of African religions with a universal (not local) world religion like Christianity. Of course, Christianity itself is divided into a number of different denominations which all claim to be Christian, but each of these is practiced by peoples who live in many different countries and belong to many different national groups. A Roman Catholic Christian who lives in Minneapolis, for example, takes part in the same rituals, has the same beliefs, and pays allegiance

A Masai native. The Masai are only one of about two thousand tribes in Africa.

to the same pope as a Roman Catholic who lives in Rome or a Roman Catholic who lives in Montreal. The three people see themselves as members of the same religion although they belong to different nationalities. They are Catholics *and also* American, Italian, or Canadian, as the case may be. Furthermore, converting a German to Roman Catholicism, for example, does not involve changing his or her national or ethnic identity.

Just as the social organization of African tribes varies from group to group and from region to region, so does the form that each tribal religion takes. For example, among the Kikuyu of Kenya the circumcision of young boys and girls at the age of puberty is celebrated with an elaborate and lengthy series of rituals. Unless the individual undergoes these rituals, he or she is not considered to be an adult member of the tribe. Many other East African peoples (and peoples in other parts of Africa as well) have similar ceremonies. In West Africa among the Yoruba and neighboring peoples, however, there is no puberty rite as such. Children are usually circumcised without ceremony between the ages of one and five. In Chapter 4, this diversity is considered at more length; at this point it is necessary only to recognize its existence.

VILLAGE RELIGIONS

Not only does each tribe have its own religion, but each local community practices its own variation of the tribal religion. This *local character* of primal religion is a source of its great hold over its believers in the traditional context. It is also a source of vulnerability when change sweeps over the land and the local community becomes linked to larger entities through colonial rule and international trade. In this situation the local religion no longer suffices to adequately explain and account for the new way of life of the people.

Typically, each village has its own set of priests for its cults, its own religious societies, its own diviners, and its own communal festivals. Most of these aspects of religion are simply the local manifestation of a cult or society that is part of the tribal religion. For example, while in one Yoruba village the thunder god, Shango, might be the most important deity, in another it might be Ogun, the god of iron. Often there are beliefs and ceremonies which are unique to that particular village. Some of these beliefs may be associated with the local environment. An especially striking tree or a local cave or hilltop may be thought of as the dwelling of a particular spirit, for example. Other beliefs may involve the ancestors of the villagers or the founder of the village who is honored annually in special ceremonies.

18

In all these ways, the tribal religion is adapted and tied to the particular locality. If the village is threatened by a plague or some other disaster, the gods, through divination, may order special sacrifices to be made at the gates of the village. The result is a close fit between the religion of the villagers and their everyday life and environment. Of course there are certain ceremonies which bring people from many different villages together and certain shrines which may be visited by all members of the tribe, but in a very important sense African primal religions are village religions.

THE PRIEST

This local character of primal religion is shown by the role of the priest in African religions. In modern-day Canada or the United States, the Christian priest or minister is usually a full-time religious worker who is paid by the local church but is trained and owes allegiance to the headquarters or authorities of his or her denomination. An Episcopal priest in Shaker Heights, Ohio, for example, who received his theological training in Cambridge, Massachusetts, and obeys the authority of the bishop of Cleveland, may go from one congregation to another (and thus usually from town to town) several times in the course of his career as a minister. Not unlike ministers in colonial America, however, the priest of an African cult usually supports himself by farming like everyone else in the community. He is only a part-time priest. His training is typically by apprenticeship to his predecessor. In small villages he is autonomous and is not subject to a chief priest. He remains in his village as a priest until he dies; there is no idea of a promotion to a larger cult group in another village.

Much of the worship in African primal religions does not even require the services of these part-time priests. Part of the varied responsibilities of African family heads is religious, which means that they perform priestly duties at certain times. Since the family's welfare depends on the right relationship between its members and the spirits, especially the ancestral spirits, the family head presides over the family's worship of the gods and the ancestors. If misfortune strikes the family, it is the responsibility of the family head to go and consult a diviner to see what is causing the misfortune and what must be done to rectify it.

This happened in a compound in Ibadan some years ago. A series of babies born to a woman in the compound died soon after birth. The death rate for babies is always high in traditional Africa, but this death rate was unusual. The head of the compound consulted a diviner, who performed the divination. According to the divination the deaths were the result of certain evil spirits, and further deaths could be prevented by sacrifices and by having a crocodile live in the compound. The spirit of the crocodile, if properly propitiated by sacrifices, would guard the spirits of the children from the evil spirits. This divination was made years ago but today, in the middle of the large compound there is a well about six feet deep, at the bottom of which is a sleepy-looking crocodile. The present compound head, who supervises the maintenance of the crocodile, claims that the death rate has been normal ever since the advent of the crocodile.

DIFFUSE RELIGION

Religion is a natural part of every aspect of the tribal African's daily life. Upon awakening in the morning, he or she utters a prayer to God or the Supreme Being (see Chapter 3). Libations may be poured on the ground to the gods before every meal. Many people wear charms or have them in their houses to protect them against the magical attacks of their enemies. Innumerable customs such as not walking in the heat of the sun at noontime (you may become insane), not feeding eggs to children (they will become thieves), and not telling someone the exact number of one's children (witches may hear you bragging and take one of them) have a religious basis. Each occupation, such as farming or blacksmithing, has its special schedule of sacrifices to the gods. Family worship, cult worship, religious festivals come and go. Virtually every aspect of life has its religious dimension, and every occurrence may have its religious explanation.

In this sense religion is diffused through the entire way of life of African peoples. Here is another contrast with Western society, where religion is so specialized. In North America more and more parents leave the religious training of their children to priests, ministers, rabbis, or Sunday school teachers. After all, these people are the official religious specialists! And as a result of secularization and the advance of science, much of our everyday lives is viewed as having nothing to do with the supernatural.

BUT ONE

Having looked at the diversity of African peoples and their religions, we now come to the other side of the "many but one" paradox, which is the subject of this chapter. Because these tribes share the same experience of being small-scale, "closed" societies with a simple technology, they also share a *common world view* which underlies their religious practices and beliefs.

This common world view is implicit, not explicit. That is, African peoples do not write discourses on the nature of humanity or the problem of the knowledge of God as modern theologians do. They do not consciously systematize their beliefs. Instead, they experience religious ritual, they transmit myths which explain the nature of things through stories about gods, they use proverbs which contain folk wisdom, and they consult diviners who apply the beliefs of the tribal religion to the practical dilemmas of sickness and suffering. Underlying all these teachings and experiences is an implicit philosophy. Some scholars who have studied African religions for the past decades have found that behind the various rituals, gods, practitioners, and spirits in all of these local religions lies a remarkable uniformity in the various peoples' understanding of the nature of the world, the nature of human beings and their place in the world, and the nature of evil. It is these understandings which comprise what might be called the *primal world view.* The portrayal of the traditional African way of looking at the world is a central task of this book, especially of Chapters 5 through 7.

There is one important qualification that needs to be made about the unity of the African primal world view. As just noted, the source of the common world view lies in the similar experiences shared by African peoples. The experience of the herding peoples and of the hunting and gathering peoples differs in several ways from that of the peoples who practice settled agriculture or fishing. Therefore, the generalizations that will be made from here on about African religions pertain only to the 80 percent or more of African peoples who are agriculturalists or fishermen.

Chapter 3

God, Divinities, Ancestors, and Spirits

Every religion has its modes of worship, its organizations, and its specialists. These elements make up the institutional form of the religion. Chapter 2 indicated some of the differences between the institutional form of Christianity in the United States and Canada and the institutions of African primal religion with respect to the role of the priest. In this chapter and the next, the institutional expression of the primal religions is explored in more depth, and further differences between the religious heritage of North America and that of Africa will become apparent.

It is not possible to take religion as practiced by any one African people and regard it as typical of the others. Each people has its own particular combination of the basic institutional elements common to most of the African religions. The best procedure for describing the form of the primal religions is, therefore, to consider each of the major elements separately and to say something about the distribution of these elements among the various African peoples. It should always be kept in mind, however, that in each African religion these elements are interwoven into a living whole.

SUPREME BEING

Every African people has a belief in a supreme being which is central to its religion. The Ibo call him Chukwu; the Ila, Leza; the Nuer, Kwoth; the Luo, Nyasi and the Yoruba, Olodumare. Although this Supreme Being is known by many names, the qualities attributed to him by the various peoples are quite similar. Note the common elements in the following qualities of God, taken from a number of different African religions.

The All-powerful
The Creator
The Giver of Rain and Sunshine
The Owner of All Things
The He Who Has All Power

The God of the World
The One Who Began the Forest
The One Who Does What No Other Can Do
The He Who Bends Down Even Majesties

This sense of God as the transcendent, all-powerful creator deity is very important in African thought. It is expressed most fully in the creation myths of the various African peoples who have such myths. Here are some excerpts from the creation myth of the Abaluyia people of Kenya as told to anthropologist Gunter Wagner by the elders of the Vugusu subtribe:

> The World was created by Wele xakaba, the granter and giver of all things. Before he created the whole world with everything in it, he made his own abode, heaven. To prevent heaven from falling in, he supported it all around by pillars just as the roof of a round hut is propped up by pillars . . . .

> After God had created heaven, he decided to put certain things in it. First he made the moon and put it into the sky, and then he created the sun . . . . After having created the sun and the moon, God made clouds and put them into the sky. He then created a big rooster from which lightning originates. This rooster is of reddish color and lives among the clouds. Whenever it shakes its wings there is lightning, and whenever it crows there is thunder. [Then follows an account of the creation of the stars, rain, rainbows, air and "cold air"—all this is said to have taken God two days to create.]

> Having created the sun . . . He asked himself, "For whom will the sun shine?" This led to God's decision to create the first man. The Vugusu believe that the first man was called Mwambu. Because God had created him so that he could talk and see, he needed someone to whom he could talk. God therefore created the first woman, called Sela, to be Mwambu's partner. [The creation of lakes, rivers, plants, and animals follows. The origin of cattle is described, and it is noted that cattle were given to Mwambu and Sela by God.]

> At first, Mwambu and Sela lived together without having any children, for "Mwambu did not know his wife." But later, when he knew her, she became pregnant and gave birth to a son, called Lilambo. Mwambu and Sela were very much astounded when they saw their first child. Later Sela bore another child, a daughter, whose name was Nasio . . . .

> [God completed the whole work of creation in six days. On the seventh day he rested because it was a bad day. The Vugusu have all sorts of beliefs and taboos referring to this day and the number seven.][1]

Most of the myths describe a time after the creation like a golden age, when there was no separation between humans and God and when humans were immortal. Then something is said to have happened. In the Vugusu mythology, humans became mortal when they were cursed by the chameleon after they had repeatedly refused its request for a share of their food. In Ghana, Ivory Coast, Togo, Benin, and Nigeria, myths explain the separation between humans and God in terms of humans becoming too familiar with God. One says a greedy man helped himself to too much food from heaven; another, that a woman touched the face of heaven (the sky) with a dirty hand; and still another, that a woman knocked against heaven with her pestle as she pounded grain. As a result heaven (God) moved away to its present distance.

There are a number of interesting parallels between these African creation myths and the Christian story of Creation as found in the Book of Genesis. No one knows how old the African myths are, nor where they originated. They are simply part of the oral tradition of the peoples that has been passed down the centuries by the tribal historians and religious specialists. Similar creation myths have been traced back by scholars to the ancient kingdoms of the Near East such as Babylonia, and it is not impossible that over the millenia the African myths may have been influenced by these ancient myths.

These myths establish the Supreme Being as the source of the world. He created not only humans but also the existing social order. In the past, some Westerners have described the Supreme Deity in African thought as a withdrawn, remote God who, having created the world, now leaves it to its own devices. The work of a number of scholars such as E. E. Evans-Pritchard, a British anthropologist, and E. B. Idowu, a Nigerian scholar of religion, has shown that although God in African thought is indeed transcendent, he is also immanent, that is, he is near and active in the universe.[2] As Evans-Pritchard writes about the Nuer tribe, for example, the Supreme Being Kwoth is the giver and sustainer of life. He gives both the good and the bad things of life. Violations of the fundamental rules of social life, such as incest and murder, are punished by him.

Probably the reason early students of African religion thought that God was remote was because among African peoples there is little ordered worship of God as God. Shrines to the Supreme Deity are very rare, and cults in his name are nonexistent. Instead, as we will see, the organized worship involves cults of deities, secret societies, ancestors, and so on. But among many African peoples, the Supreme Deity is called upon directly in their prayers, especially in their moments of personal need. Direct prayer to God is more common in West Africa than among the Bantu-speaking peoples in central Africa where individuals turn to God only as a last resort when the ancestors and hero-gods have failed. British missionary John Taylor tells of the leader of a hunting expedition in Malawi. After two unsuccessful weeks the leader exclaimed, "I am tired of asking the spirits. Let us pray to God."[3]

It is worth noting that African peoples believed in a supreme being long before Christian missionaries arrived with their concept of God. But while the African's God was an all-powerful creator with a concern for justice like the Christian God, he typically manifested himself through intermediates like the divinities, which will be considered next in this chapter. It is in this sense that African religions are polytheistic—that is, they are based on a belief in, and worship of, many gods—although some scholars would prefer to say that African religions represent a "diffused monotheism."

THE DIVINITIES

The presence of a pantheon of divinities is common in many African religions though it is by no means universal. Such divinities are generally absent in the religions of East African peoples, while they are an important part of the religion of a number of West African peoples. Divinities are deities typically ascribed a particular function or associated with a particular aspect of nature. For example, among the Yoruba, Sopono is the god of smallpox and insanity, Ogun is the god of iron, Orisha-oko is the goddess of the farm, Shango the god of thunder, and so on. The divinities are hierarchically ordered, with some being ascribed more power than others, and are the subject of many myths. Similar pantheons characterized Greek, Roman, and Norse religion.

The supremacy of God over all other spiritual forces, including the divinities, is what led E. B. Idowu to label African religions as a form of diffused monotheism rather than polytheism. African peoples believe that the divinities receive their power from God, the Supreme Being, and are his emissaries on earth. Each divinity has its cult and its devotees who regularly worship the divinity. The devotees order their lives according to the injunctions of the cult and, by so doing, participate in the power of the divinity. Generally people inherit the worship of a particular divinity because of their occupation (for example, Yoruba blacksmiths, because they work with iron, are automatically Ogun worshippers) or because they may be "called" by a divinity to worship him or her. (Some of the divinities are female.) In the latter case, a diviner will tell a person who is sick or suffering from a series of misfortunes that the suffering is caused by a particular divinity who wants the person to worship him or her.

Each cult worships its divinity at regular intervals and also at an annual festival where the devotees may be joined by many others who wish to honor the divinity and to receive its blessings. In West Africa and central Africa the divinities are often represented by wood carvings which people worship or revere much as Christians revere the cross. Obviously, as with the cross, it is not the object itself which is worshipped or revered, but the spirit of the divinity which is associated with the carving. A special feature of divinity worship in West Africa involves the priest and/or some of the devotees becoming possessed by the spirit of the divinity. It is believed that in this way the divinity more directly manifests itself to the believers—that it is literally among them. The closest analogy in the United States to this kind of possession is the Pentecostal practice of becoming filled by God and "speaking in tongues."

THE ANCESTORS

The ancestors are an important dimension of African primal religions all over the continent, although the ancestral cult is of greater importance among some peoples than others. The general belief is that the dead continue their existence as "shades" or spirits and that they possess the power to affect the living, particularly when newly dead or if the dead person were an especially powerful person while alive. Alexis Kagame, an African philosopher, has expressed this in an epigram: "The living man is happier than the departed because he is alive. But the departed are more powerful."[4]

In North America respect for the dead is shown at funerals, and many people continue to honor the dead by bringing flowers to graves at certain times. In the Roman Catholic religion a few dead people who lived exemplary lives are recognized by the church as saints, and there is the recognition that the saints may be enabled by God to work miracles. There are also North American folk beliefs about ghosts and, of course, the annual Halloween festival which in a sense is the secularized version of All Hallow's Eve, the night before All Saints' Day. So there are similarities between African ancestor worship and North American religions. What, then, is the difference?

The difference lies in the African's greater sense of continuity between the living and the dead. For an African the ancestors, especially the immediate ones, really "live" and manifest themselves in this world in various ways. The family includes both the living and the spirits of the dead. Professor Idowu explains the nature and meaning

27

of the relationship of the ancestors and the living very well in the following quotation.

> The deceased are truly members of the families on earth; but they are no longer of the same fleshly order as those who are still actually living in the flesh on earth . . . . Because they have crossed the borderland between this world and the super-sensible world, entering and living in the latter, they have become freed from the restrictions imposed by the physical world. They can now come to abide with their folk on earth invisibly, to aid or hinder them . . . . To some extent, they are intermediaries between Deity or the divinities and their own children; this is a continuation of their earthly function whereby they combined the headships of the families or communities with the office of family or community priests or priestesses.[5]

Idowu goes on to point out that in Africa the living father or mother has the power to bless or to curse the undertakings of their children. How much more, then, does the ancestor have such power!

Ancestor worship takes many different forms in the primal religions. In Chapter 1 a manifestation of ancestor worship among the Yoruba was described—the Egungun festival. Often the ancestors are called upon daily as with the Ibo of eastern Nigeria whose morning ritual begins with this invocation: "Chukwu (Deity), come and eat kola-nut; Ala (Earth Goddess), come and eat kola-nut; Ndiche

(top) Carved figures of gods.
(bottom) Ancestral shrine in the courtyard of the
palace of the king of Benin. Note the carved elephant
tusks, and the bamboo staffs representing the
ancestors of the king.

(Ancestors), come and eat kola-nut." (A kola nut is a bitter-tasting nut which is broken and offered to honored guests as a gesture of hospitality by the Ibo.) It is common for people to spill a little of their food or drink on the ground as a way of sharing with the ancestors.

In African societies with kings, however, the ancestor cult of the kings assumes a particular importance. In most of theses societies the living king has sacred attributes. He is believed to possess special powers, and his performance of the communal rituals of the gods and ancestors is essential to the well-being of the kingdom. The worship of the kingly ancestors is often among his most important duties. In one of the courtyards of the palace of the oba (king) of Benin, a kingdom on the Atlantic coast in southern Nigeria, is a special shrine. On it is a cluster of beautifully wrought brass figures and bells as well as a number of blackened staffs which lean against the mud wall surrounding the courtyard. Each of these staffs represents one of the present oba's predecessors. Every year an important week-long festival is held to commemorate the royal ancestors. The involvement of the entire community in the festival reinforces the unity of the kingdom, and the propitiation of the royal ancestors ensures its prosperity during the coming year.

THE SPIRITS

The word *animism* is often used to describe African primal religions. The word suggests a belief that there is a soul (anima) or spirit in every being and object. One must be careful in applying this label to African religions, however, because, as we have seen, these religions have strong beliefs in the Supreme Being and in the ancestors. Since African religions involve much more than a belief in animistic spirits, animism is only one aspect of the primal religions.

The divinities and the ancestors are spirits too, of course, but they are "domesticated," to use Idowu's term. The ancestors are part of a human family and the divinities are incorporated into cults while the spirits are not as clearly defined. The spirits take a much more indefinite form. Some of them are generalized ancestral "shades"; some are spirits associated with particular animals or other natural objects such as trees, mountains, rivers, or other parts of nature.

For example among the Badyaranke of Senegal an invisible powerful force called *koase* is believed to inhabit certain stones which are usually found near tree roots. This force reveals itself to an individual who becomes the custodian of a shrine which is consulted by people who wish to use the koase. William Simmons, an anthropologist who studied the Badyaranke, writes that anyone making a request must do so in terms of an equitable contract. For example, a person might promise to pay the shrine a chicken for a safe journey or a cow in exchange for the death of an enemy. The force within the shrine is said to be visible to seers and to visit the village occasionally as an animal or a whirlwind.

Another kind of spirit is the Yoruba *abiku* spirit. People of the Yoruba tribe believe that abiku spirits sometimes deliberately enter a woman's womb and are born as apparently normal children only to die shortly after birth. They will torment a woman by repeating this process time after time. When a diviner-healer has ascertained that this is the cause of the woman's failure to raise a healthy child, there are various rituals that can be performed to prevent the particular abiku spirit from reappearing or, in the case of an infant that is newly born but still alive, to "tie " the spirit to the earth so that the child will grow up.

Other spirits, especially those associated with major geographical features, may be the object of communal ritual. Kenneth Little, a British anthropologist, has described the annual sacrifices which a town in Upper Mende in Sierra Leone makes to the spirit of the river on which the town is situated. This river regularly overflows its banks during September. According to Little this is interpreted by a diviner as a warning that the conduct of the people has angered the spirit dwelling in the river and that the whole country will be flooded if the spirit is not propitiated. The entire countryside contributes food to be cooked for the sacrifice which takes place at a spot near the river where the spirit lives. The lowering of the flooding is taken as a sign that the spirit has been successfully appeased.[6]

Chapter 4

Festivals, Rites of Passage, and Diviner-Healers

This chapter continues the examination of some of the elements which make up the institutional form of African primal religions. The three elements discussed here—festivals, rites of passage, and diviner-healers—are important and very widespread components of the primal religions. They differ markedly in the level of communal involvement which they entail, however. At one extreme are the festivals which typically involve the entire community in a common act of worship. The diviner-healer is at the other extreme. He is consulted by individuals who face particular problems such as sickness, and he ministers to their needs much as a Western doctor treats individual patients. The various rites of passage lie in between. Some of them, such as the initiation rites, have a communal involvement while other rites, such as naming ceremonies and marriage, primarily involve kinship groups. Taken together these three elements, which are found in most of the African primal religions, help us understand the diversity and complexity of these religions.

FESTIVALS

Every world religion has a cycle of religious celebrations or festivals. The Christian year, for example, is marked by the great festivals of Christmas and Easter as well as many minor ones such as All Saints' Day and Pentecost. In the United States there are also important civil festivals such as Thanksgiving, Memorial Day, and Independence Day, which are celebrated by all Americans. These latter festivals, while officially secular, take on certain nondenominational sacred overtones. In traditional African societies a round of festivals is often an important aspect of religion. Nowhere is this more the case than among the Kalabari.

The Kalabari people live in some thirty villages in a corner of the vast delta created by the Niger River where it meets the sea in southeastern Nigeria. Most of the villages have always made their living by fishing, but in the past four hundred years a couple of villages near the ocean abandoned this occupation for trade with Europe in slaves and palm oil. This shift in their economic base affected the political structure of these villages but in most other respects, including their religion, they are no different than their fishing counterparts.

The Kalabari villages are built on those rare dry portions of land which are raised above the generally swampy delta landscape. Although the thatch-roofed houses are set close together to make the most of the limited amount of dry land, at the heart of every Kalabari village is a large, open central square which is used for sessions of the village assembly and for the many festivals which are an important part of Kalabari religious life. Robin Horton, a British anthropologist, has studied the Kalabari for many years and has described their festivals in a fascinating booklet entitled *The Gods as Guests*.[1]

According to Horton, the Kalabari have two distinct systems of gods. One of these systems is relatively abstract and involves the female deity Tamuno, who is responsible for creation, and the male deity, So, who is thought to be responsible for the control of creation. The second system of gods is made up of the Village Heroes, the Water People, and the Dead. These latter gods are associated with particular human and natural conditions and are given what Horton calls a "full-blooded sense of personality." All of them have a rich mythology describing their origin and feats.

The Village Heroes are figures who are believed to have once lived in the village and to have excelled in some particular activity. These figures, the myths say, eventually tired of living on earth and vanished, leaving behind them the instructions that prayer and offering should be made to them and the promise that they would continue to look after the community. The Water People are concerned with the control of the capricious aspects of nature that are of vital importance to a fishing people, such as the movements of the fish and the level of the water in a particular area. The Dead are the spirits of the ancestors who are believed to continue to participate in a society similar to that of the living Kalabari.

It is only for the second set of gods that the Kalabari have developed the ritual dramatizations which mark their cycle of festivals. Unlike Tamuno and So, who are faceless gods of form and process, the Water People, Village Heroes, and Dead have earthly personalities which are ritually dramatized. Human actors using mime, masquerade, or possession portray the personality of these gods, and in this way the gods are brought as "guests" into the village. Festivals for Village Heroes and the Dead are held periodically, following which the Ekine Society, a male religious group, stages a sequence of forty or more Water People masquerades. Each of the Water People masquerades lasts for a day or two. As the interval between the masquerades is anywhere from a couple of days to some months, the entire Water People cycle may take years to perform!

The Water People sequence is a fascinating one. The personal characteristics of the various Water People range across the spectrum of human personality types. Among the Water People Horton describes is the Igbo spirit, "a lascivious good-time 'bluffer' who can never resist using up all the family funds in buying the favors of a woman when his father sends him up-river to buy yams—in masquerade he continuously falters in the serious business of dancing and rushes off for a lecherous advance upon some pretty girl in the audience." Another is Igoni, "the self-pitying old woman whose own troubles are insufficient and who, therefore, takes up everyone else's sorrows—in masquerade she wanders mournfully about alternately singing sadly about her own misfortunes and those of members of the audience."[2] Other Water People manifest themselves as more powerful and ruthless, sometimes striking out unpredictably with sharp machetes at the young men who dare to stand near the man who is possessed by the Water Spirit. This alternating pattern of comic interludes and moments of tension is a characteristic of Kalabari ritual.

These festivals are, in Horton's words, "an intimate blend of religion and recreation." In many of them there is a lighthearted quality which is the opposite of the solemnity which most of us associate with religious ritual. The Kalabari see these as entertainments of the gods. Just as important living men would be entertained and their support solicited, so the gods are entertained—but on a much more lavish scale as befits their status. They are occasions of joy, either in thanksgiving for blessings that the community has already received or in a confident assurance that the gods will continue to ensure the prosperity of the village. When the complex ritual action is analyzed, it is seen to depict the values and beliefs of Kalabari society. Each action, no matter how bizarre it may seem to the outsider, has meaning in the context of Kalabari culture. Life in a small village inevitably is marred by strife and tension at times. Communal participation in festivals such as these helps to reintegrate the villagers at the same time that it reinforces the values and traditions embodied in their religion.

RITES OF PASSAGE

What do birth, the attainment of puberty, marriage, and death have in common? They are turning points in the lives of individuals, times when a person shifts from one important status to another. At birth the individual becomes a member of a family; through initiation at the time of puberty the individual shifts from the status of a child to the status of an adult; marriage legitimates the creation of a family of one's own; and at death the individual becomes an ancestor. Furthermore, each of these turning points has consequences for other people besides the individual. The individual's community and, most especially, his or her family are also involved. It should not be surprising that events such as these are often marked by religious ritual, or rites of passage, by African peoples. The ritual defines the meaning of the event and helps the individual and his or her family mark the irreversible transition that has taken place.

In Africa the newborn child is welcomed into the family through the *naming ceremony*. Noel King, who teaches religious studies at the University of California, Santa Cruz, has described this ceremony for the Ga, a people who live in the coastal region of Ghana near Accra. Very early before dawn on the morning of the eighth day after birth, the baby is carried from its mother's family's house where it was born to the father's family's house where relatives and friends have gathered. The child is lifted up toward the heavens and then is laid down gently, naked, under the eaves of the house. A little water is poured on the roof of the house and allowed to drip on the baby like rain. These acts symbolize the presentation of the child to the heavens, to earth, and to water. Then the sponsor, usually a virtuous old person of the same sex as the child, prays blessings upon the child. According to King, the sponsor:

> calls upon the elements and the ancestors to witness the coming of this new member and to receive him or her as their own. They refer to the tribal virtues and their own, praying that the child may become a partaker of them . . . . More blessings are called by other members of the baby's family on both father and mother's sides. Libation is poured to the dead and then all drink. The child has entered into his place as a member of the community and is now called by his Ga name which is laid down by a complicated process of inheritance.[3]

Among a number of West African peoples, including the Ga and the Yoruba, the transition to adulthood is not marked by special ceremony, and circumcision is performed at an early age without much ritual. Among many other African peoples, however, *initiation rites* occupy a central place in their culture. This is especially true in East Africa. In these societies, unless a boy or girl has undergone this ceremony, which may involve months or even years of seclusion from the village in the company of adult ritual masters and the other initiates, the person is not recognized as an adult and cannot marry.

Generally the initiation rites take place about the age of puberty. A group of uninitiated children of the appropriate age are brought together in a sacred place set aside for this purpose away from the village. The children live together away from their families under the control of the elders who have the responsibility for the ritual. Part of the rite almost always involves the circumcision of the children. This operation, which is carried out without the benefit of anesthesia, is naturally very painful, and much praise is given those initiates who endure it with fortitude. The joint endurance of this ordeal creates a strong bond among the initiates which continues throughout their lives and prepares them for the suffering and hardships of life. Before and after the circumcision rite the initiates are instructed in the traditions of the tribe, in the performance of the various rituals involved in the process of initiation, and in the appropriate performance of sexual and matrimonial roles. Some of these rituals are performed in the camp away from the community while others are performed publicly. To the outsider who lacks a deep understanding of the culture of the people, these rites seem very confusing and chaotic. Anthropologists who study these rites, however, find that they embody a coherent collection of symbolism. The words of the songs, the actions of the participants, and even the colors of the materials used all symbolize, in various complex ways, the death as children and rebirth as adults which is accomplished by the rites and the adult ideals to which the initiates should aspire. The blessings of the gods and ancestors are always invoked.

Marriage and *funerals,* the remaining two rites of passage to be considered, are universally celebrated by African peoples just as they are in Western culture. The details of the ceremonies vary from people to people, of course, and one very interesting class project would be to compare the marriage or funeral rituals of two different African peoples to see what they have in common and how they differ. Here space allows only a few generalizations about these important rites.

1. In Africa the rituals for both marriage and funerals often have several stages that take place over long periods of time. In some societies rites that mark betrothal occur years before the marriage. Rituals which take place months or years after death are common among many other African peoples, and death rituals are usually very complex.

2. The rituals of marriage and funerals are performed by members of the family, not by nonfamily religious specialists as in Western culture. In marriage the parents of the couple play an important

role, while in funerals the brothers of the deceased and the eldest son may well have the important ritual roles.

3. The proper performance of the funeral rites are thought to be of extreme spiritual importance because of the potential for the power of the dead to bring bad luck. In a sense the dead are dependent upon the living properly performing the rituals so as to put them at rest, and the living are dependent upon the dead to link the family with the spiritual power which the ancestors command. When performed correctly, it is believed that the funeral ceremony puts the spirit of the dead at rest and ensures the all-important continuity between the living and the dead.

4. The importance of kinship relations in African traditional society was pointed out in Chapter 2. In these societies, individualism is viewed with suspicion and membership in the family group assumes a crucial importance. Marriage, in this context, involves an alliance between kinship groups. Since most African peoples have unilineal descent and trace their ancestry through either the father's or the mother's line, the betrothal and marriage ceremonies symbolize the fact that one group loses a member and the other gains a member. For example, if the people are patrilineal and patrilocal, the new wife leaves her kinship group and joins that of her husband. Her children belong to the husband's group, and if there is a divorce the husband keeps the children. In this context the widespread custom of the "bride price" makes sense. The bride is not being "bought." Rather the "bride price" involves the husband's group making a gift to the wife's group in symbolic compensation for their loss. The marriage ceremony itself sometimes symbolizes the bride's removal from her group to her husband's through a ritual capture of the bride. I will never forget how puzzled I was the first time I saw a Yoruba marriage because the bride appeared to be so unhappy. She was almost in tears, unlike the "radiant" bride that is the norm in Western culture. I quickly learned that she was simply showing the feelings that are expected in her culture because, after all, she was leaving her kinship group permanently to become a member of her husband's group, and an expression of joy at such an event would be in bad taste.

DIVINER-HEALERS

The last of the institutional elements to be considered in this chapter is one of the most important. This is the diviner-healer, the person whose priestly role centers on the interpretation of the spiritual situation of individuals and the cure of psychological and physical ailments. Before beginning this analysis of the diviner-healer, consider the Western stereotype of him as the witch doctor. What image does the term *witch doctor* have for you? Perhaps you think of someone involved in the black arts, someone steeped in superstition, someone performing meaningless mumbo jumbo in front of credulous savages. Many Westerners have such an image of the diviner-healer. As you will see, it is an inaccurate image.

Diviner-healers are basically spiritual counselors and physicians. Individuals will typically bring a wide variety of requests to these priests. Perhaps they are going on a journey and wish to know if a particular time is propitious for the journey. Perhaps they have been unsuccessful in farming or trade and wish to know why and what they can do about it. Perhaps they have a sickness that is bothering them. Perhaps they fear that their enemies are planning to work magic against them and wish to seek spiritual protection. They may have had an unsettling dream that requires interpretation. These are all situations of uncertainty, of course, and in such situations the adherents of primal religions typically feel the need to call upon the spiritual resources of the diviner-healer. These are real human needs which are recognized as legitimate in African cultures and which the diviner-healer is believed to be able to help. Therefore, among most African peoples diviner-healers deal primarily in "white," or protective, magic, not "black," or destructive, magic. They are a force for good in the community, therefore, and not a solitary antisocial practitioner of the black arts. Rather than being steeped in superstition, the diviner-healers are steeped in the religious traditions of their people. Through long periods of apprenticeship they have acquired the accumulated wisdom of their people.

Among the Yoruba, for example, the diviner-healers are called *babalawos,* a word which means "father of secrets" when translated literally. One of the Yoruba deities, Ifa, is especially associated with divination, and the babalawos are priests of this cult although they are consulted by members of all cults. Individuals will bring their problems to a babalawo whose reputation they respect. Without even asking about the nature of the problem the babalawo will perform the process of divination which will reveal the nature of the problem, its cause, and its cure. Babalawos also make divination for the entire community at the beginnings of festivals and at times of national crisis such as during an epidemic or war. In addition to their activities as diviner-healers, which is their principal occupation, babalawos are also herbalists. Clients may come to them just for their herbal remedies without divination.

The principle behind divination is to permit spiritual powers to give guidance through the outcomes of operations which involve chance. Often the answer is simply yes or no, as when the head of a chicken is cut off and its final position after flapping around in its death agonies is noted. If it lies on its back, the answer is yes; if it lies on its stomach, the answer is no. There is no way to predict the final position, which is purely the result of chance. But the belief is that when this form of divination is performed in the context of invoking a certain god or spirit, the final position is caused by that god or spirit and is a divine message.

There are numerous methods of divination practiced by African peoples. The method cited above is an exceedingly simple one. The answer is either yes or no. If the issue is complex, such a method may have to be repeated a number of times before the answer to a question such as "What is the cause of my brother's death?" can be answered. Another method which is fairly widespread involves the priest or priestess becoming possessed by a god who then uses the diviner as an oracle. Still other methods of divination give answers which require interpretation. The method used by the Yoruba babalawos is one of the most interesting and complex of these methods.

The babalawo takes a handful of sixteen palm nuts in his left hand (they are about the size of acorns) and grabs them with his right hand so that one or two remain. He counts the nuts that remain in his left hand. If two remain, he makes one line in the wood dust on the carved divining board which lies on the ground in front of him. If one

(top) Young men in western Kenya. They are painted white as part of the initiation ceremony which allows them to be accepted as adult members of their tribe. (bottom) A Yoruba diviner-healer attempts to cure one of his people of an illness.

remains, he makes two lines. This process is repeated eight times until a pattern of single and double lines in two columns of four results. There is a total of 256 different patterns of lines which are possible from the eight different random occurrences, and each of these patterns has a name. The babalawo has spent years of apprenticeship to a senior babalawo learning these names and also memorizing the series of stories and songs associated with each of these patterns. This feat of memory in learning thousands of verses is roughly comparable to memorizing the New Testament!

Up to this point the result is entirely by chance. Now the diviner-healer begins to recite the three or more sets of verses, called odus, that he has memorized for that particular pattern. These odus include myths, folktales, praise names, incantations, songs, proverbs, and even riddles. Together they constitute the unwritten scriptures of the Yoruba. As the diviner recites the odus, the client decides which one is most appropriate for his or her purpose. The answer to the client's problem lies in the prediction and the required sacrifice described in the odu which is chosen. Many of the odus are full of complex allusions and have no obvious meaning, while others, such as the Ifa verse reprinted below, are much more direct an easy to interpret.

A young man who had been unable to sleep well for several nights because of nightmares came to a diviner-healer in the Yoruba town of Ife. The pattern named ogbe irosun came up in the divination, and among the verses the diviner recited was the following short one which the young man took as the answer to his problem.

"Ogbe sees Camwood[a]; Camwood sees the priest" was the one who cast Ifa for Rascal when he was dreaming about his father.

> I saw my father today:
> Father of leopard,
> Father of cat,
> Father of panther,
> Father come from heaven to help me;
> The child's father does not refuse to help his child,
> The Child's Father.

Ifa says someone has forgotten his father and that if he does not take care of his father there will be no one on earth to take care of him.[b] One ram and three shillings six pence is the sacrifice.[c] When

---

a) Camwood is the red bark of a certain tree which is mixed into a paste and applied to the skin of women as makeup.
b) To "forget" a father means to neglect the worship of one's father as an ancestor. If someone does not worship one's father, this line suggests, who will worship that person when he becomes an ancestor?
c) Roughly the equivalent of fifty cents in today's currency. The money sacrifice is given to the babalawo and comprises his payment.

this sacrifice has been made, this person should go and sacrifice the ram to his father; but if the father is still alive, he should sacrifice the ram to his father's head[d] so that the way to success may be clear for him. Something of the person concerned will spoil[e] completely if he does not take care of his father, whether he is on earth or in heaven.[4]

The young man interpreted his nightmares as caused by his deceased father who was annoyed because of the young man's failure to make the regular sacrifices associated with the ancestor cult. By giving the three shillings six pence to the diviner and sacrificing the ram, he believed that the ancestral spirit would be appeased and his night-mares would cease.

The role of the diviner-healer is a central one in many of the African primal religions. Certain diviners gain such outstanding reputations that clients will come many miles to consult them. The diviner collects fees from his clients but he operates by a system of professional ethics which, among the Yoruba at least, requires him to perform divination without collecting a fee for clients who are too poor to pay it. The next three chapters explore the beliefs which lie behind the work of the diviners and the other practices which make up the primal religions. These beliefs, or the primal world view, continue to be widely held. It is interesting to note that of all the elements of the African primal religions, the diviner-healers alone have been relatively unaffected by the impact of Islam and Christianity. They continue to flourish and to be consulted in times of crisis by many Muslims and Christians as well as by traditionalists.

---

d) The meaning of this line will be explained in the next chapter.
e) That is, things will go wrong; the person will have bad luck.

Chapter 5

The Nature and Destiny of Humanity

All religions seek to provide an understanding of the nature of humanity, of how the world runs, and of the meaning of evil and misfortune; African religions are no exception. Chapter 2 introduced the idea of a common world view which underlies the varied religious practices and beliefs of the African primal religions. The next three chapters examine the answers this world view provides for these fundamental questions. Although presented at a level of high generality which admits of some exceptions, the principles that are outlined have wide applicability across the continent.

A portion of the Abaluyia creation myth was given in Chapter 3, and it was noted there that the various African creation myths describe the initial relationship between humans and God as one of closeness, where humans were immortal. This was indeed a paradise much like the one that Adam and Eve enjoyed in the biblical Creation story. Just as Adam and Eve sinned and were expelled from the Garden of Eden, so in the African creation myths a separation of God and humans came about. This separation is sometimes caused by people breaking a taboo; in other myths it is explained as the result of an accidental occurrence beyond the control of humans. Because of the separation, humans have become mortal and die. Thus, humans are portrayed by these myths as beings who are created by God and are especially favored by God over the other animals and yet who live in separation from God.

African religions accept this separation as a given. There are no myths that suggest a solution or reversal of this separation. Stated in other terms, these religions are not religions of salvation. They do not offer a radical solution to humanity's separation from God as Christianity does through faith in Jesus Christ, as Islam does through belief in Allah and Muhammad, his prophet, or as Buddhism does through the attainment of Nirvana. In African religions, people live their lives in the context of human frailty and death without the assurance of deliverance from this condition either in this life or in the next.

What, then, is the destiny of humanity in the African primal world view? Unlike Christianity, Islam, and Buddhism, which offer a life or existence which transcends death, the destiny of humanity in African religion is primarily this-worldly. *The primary object of life is to fulfill one's life's destiny in this life.* This includes attaining a respected position in the community, having children, living to an old age, and dying of natural causes. There are many threats to this destiny, as we shall see in succeeding chapters, and African religion provides the spiritual resources that are necessary to overcome these threats.

The notion of a "life's destiny" is an important one in this context. Many African peoples believe that each individual is given a particular destiny by the creator before birth. In an important sense a person's destiny is part of his or her character; it is something that is part of the very essence of a person's being. In Ghana it is believed that destiny is determined by the manner in which the new living being takes leave of God before birth. According to this belief, a being will go into the world and choose all that is agreeable such as well-being, long life, and prosperity or it may choose "grief, rags, and dark cloth." Of course, the memory of the choice is erased upon birth. Among the Basongye, a people who live in the grasslands of eastern Zaire, it is believed that the creator designates the person's life span at birth, and some Basongye today even believe that all the details of life are predestined.

Destiny therefore involves the idea of predestination, but predestination is *relative,* not absolute, in the primal world view. One's destiny can be adversely affected by witches or one's enemies, for example, and conversely an individual can take ritual action through divination and sacrifice to overcome what is apparently a bad destiny. A person's lot in life is by no means totally predetermined, and while there is a certain amount of fatalism in the African world view, it is fatalism of the last resort. As one African expressed it, "Suppose you want a certain woman, but when you ask her to marry you she refuses. You try and try with all the ways you know, but she will not change her mind. Well, sometime you have to say, 'I can't get her. I'll just have to give up. It is fate.'"

Sickness and death are obviously a threat to one's life's destiny except in the case of old people, where death is a natural culmination to one's earthly lot and the beginning of a further existence as an ancestor. Thus, in the primal world view sickness is a religious problem as well as a physical problem, and much of the ritual involves the cure of sickness or the prevention of sickness and other misfortunes. There is an unabashed concern for spiritual help with the problems of life. The basic message of most of the traditional prayers of the Akan people in

Ghana is: "Bring us children, health to all of us." The same can be said for most of the other African peoples. Although this is a self-regarding perspective on life, it should not be thought of as selfish because in the primal world view, as we shall see in the next chapter, the individual's well-being is important for the peace and well-being of the entire community.

THE MULTIPLE SELF

Central to the African view of personality is the concept of the "multiple self," each aspect of which is believed to have an external character. In Africa the various components of the self are pictured as separate entities rather loosely held together, each having a different source and a different function. Sometimes in the literature on the subject these are spoken of as "souls"; and although beliefs about these vary among African peoples, British missionary John Taylor has identified four of these as widespread among African people.[1] One component of the self is the "life-soul," which is the source of instinct and impulse. The life-soul may save a man from danger by giving him a sudden feeling that an enemy is about to attack. The "individual-soul," or "personality-soul," is the essence of the person as an individual. After death this is the element of the self which lives on as a shade or ancestor. Some peoples say that every person has a third component, an "ancestor-soul," which is the individual's personal participation in the collective personality of the people. The life-soul is individual, whereas the ancestor-soul is corporate.

A fourth component of the individual's personality is the "trans-cendent-soul," which signifies that which a person has in common with God himself and receives directly from God. The British anthro-pologist John Middleton has described it for the Lugbara of Uganda, who call this component *tali.* "It refers to the manifestation of the power of God in his transcendent, creative, 'good' aspect. . . . The tali, however, is not associated with man as an ancestor . . . and goes to dwell with God in the Sky [after death]."[2] The Yoruba word for the transcendent-soul is *ori,* or "head." The physical head is a symbol of the person's destiny which is received from God at birth. The trans-cendent-soul, or ori, is an active force guiding the individual in his or her life.

THE EXTERNAL DIMENSION OF THE SELF

Westerners tend to think of the aspects of their personality as internal, as something inside themselves. Africans, on the other hand, view the multiple self as *having important external qualities*. They see its parts as acting upon the individual from "beyond" that individual, so to speak. For example, bad luck may be ascribed to the working of one's transcendent-soul. Parts of the self are also believed to leave the body at certain times. The African understanding of dreams, for instance, is that they are a real experience in which the individual-soul goes forth to these encounters while other elements of the self sleep.

This concept of externality, which is difficult for us Westerners to understand, is perhaps most clearly shown in the Yoruba belief that the ori (head) acts as the individual's guardian or protector. Consider the advice that Yorubas traditionally give to a new bride on going to her husband's house: "Take ori along, do not take beauty along; beauty remains in a day; it is ori that abides with one in the husband's house." This explains why a person might want to sacrifice to his father's head if the father is still alive, as the odu quoted in the preceding chapter required. The ori, like the deities or the ancestors, is a separate entity with whom one wants to be on good terms so that it may bring good luck. The father's ori may affect the son and a husband's ori may affect his wife so that she may be advised, when experiencing difficulty, to sacrifice to it. About the closest counterpart to this in the English language is the vague idea of a "guardian angel."

Another example of the externalizing aspects of the self which Westerners see as internal is the African view of anger. In Africa there is a universal belief that anger can take on a life of its own. It continues to be a part of the self, but it also moves out beyond the person's individual presence and becomes an independent agent which can act on that person or on the object of the anger. "Anger," says an Akan proverb, "is like a stranger, it does not stay in one house." A father, it is believed, may cause his child to become sick simply by brooding in anger at his son's insults. The same kind of belief lies behind the African notion that a person's shadow is an extension of his self and that knowledge of his or her name may give an enemy power over the person. Likewise many Africans believe that nail-clippings, personal possessions, and even footprints of a person may be used by his or her enemies to gain magical power over that person. Beliefs very similar to these are practiced by some West Indians of African ancestry, particularly in Haiti, and are called *voodoo*. They are part of these peoples' African heritage.

As you can see, in order to comprehend the African concept of personality, we must enter a world that is very strange to Westerners. We must loosen the tight boundaries drawn around human personalities so that we can perceive the African notion of the interrelatedness of selves. As John Taylor has succinctly expressed: "In Africa 'I think, therefore I am' is replaced by 'I participate, therefore I am.'"[3]

THE LIVING-DEAD

The role that ancestors play in African religion has been mentioned at several points in this book. The following discussion of the African concepts of the living-dead and reincarnation will consider these beliefs about the dead and about ancestors more systematically and relate them to the this-worldly emphasis of African religion.

After death it is believed that the person's individual-soul lives on for a considerable period of time. John Mbiti, a Kenyan theologian, has coined the term *living-dead* to refer to this state of being, while in the anthropological literature the term *shade* is often used. Mbiti's term is a very apt description of the ancestors because, as pointed out in Chapter 3, the primal world view emphasizes the *continuity* between the living and the dead. To be sure, the living-dead do occupy their own separate world, but African thought does not describe this world in much detail. It is simply a shadowy world which is thought to be very similar to the world of the living. What African thought does emphasize is the ongoing character of the new relationship between the living-dead and the living, between the ancestors and the relatives who are alive. The living-dead have spiritual power and act as intermediaries between the family and the spirits and guardians of family affairs and the traditions of the people.

This is quite different from the Western Christian understanding of death and human destiny. First of all, with rare exceptions there is no conception of final judgment in African thought. The dead person's life is not evaluated and the quality of his or her life after death is not determined by the quality of his or her life on earth. In African thought, as we shall see, evil acts are believed to have negative consequences on life in this world. Secondly, therefore, African thought lacks concepts of heaven and hell. There is simply one place where the dead go, and that place is not described in terms of punishment or reward. There is, however, the idea that the dead have to make the transition to that place and that if the appropriate funeral rituals are not carried out the spirit of the dead person may not find "rest." Note that this is not the "fault" of the dead person but of the living members of his or her family.

Third, while in the Christian view the dead individually receive their reward for eternity, in the African world view personal immortality is temporary. As long as there are people alive who knew the dead person, he or she continues as a living-dead. According to John Mbiti, after several generations have passed and the last person who knew him or her has died, the living-dead individual becomes a spirit and enters a state of collective immortality.

> It has lost its personal name as far as human beings are concerned, and with it goes also the human personality. It is now an "it" and no longer a "he" or "she"; it is now one of myriads of spirits who have lost their humanness. This, for all practical purposes, is the final destiny of the human soul. Man is ontologically destined to lose his humanness but gain his full spiritness.[4]

REINCARNATION

Many African peoples believe that part of the self of a living-dead person may be reincarnated in a newborn child. Among the Yoruba the reincarnation takes place within the family and is recognized when divination reveals that the ori, or transcendent-soul, of a very young baby shares the ori of a dead grandfather or grandmother. It is then said that the ancestor has "turned to be a child." In a more specific sense, if a baby boy is born immediately after the death of his grandfather or a baby girl after the death of her grandmother, he or she is given a special name. For boys this name is Babatunde, which means "father has returned." For girls the name is Iyatunde, "mother has returned."

It is believed that only a few ancestors are reincarnated in this way, although some of them may be reincarnated in more than one individual. Furthermore, the ancestors so reincarnated continue simultaneously as living-dead! How can this be? The logic behind these ideas can be understood by drawing on the ideas of the multiple self and the external dimension of the self. Reincarnation is simply another expression of the continuity between the living and the dead in African cultures. Just as we sometimes look at a child and see characteristics of parents or grandparents in that child, so Africans see what E. B. Idowu calls "dominant lineage characteristics" reappearing in the new generation. Their way of conceptualizing this is to see it as part of the ancestor's self (the transcendent-soul) reappearing in the transcendent-soul of the young child. Since the idea of the self having external aspects while continuing to be the self is part of their world view, this partial incarnation is not incompatible with the continued existence of the ancestor as a living-dead. The African partial reincarnation is very different from the "total" reincarnation in Buddhist thought, however, where the destiny of a human being is to go from one incarnation to another until the person is able to break out of the cycle by attaining Nirvana.

Chapter 6

Forces

In the fall of 1975, Gallup polltakers conducted a survey regarding belief in astrology in the United States. According to their findings 22 percent of the adult population in the United States, or 32 million people, believe in astrology. What does this have to do with the African primal religions? It shows that there are a large number of Americans who apparently believe that their lives are influenced by cosmic forces—forces other than those natural forces which "obey" the laws of physics and chemistry.

Astrology is based on the belief that the planets and stars exert a special influence on the lives of humans. It holds that human character and life progress are determined by the particular configuration of heavenly bodies at the time of each individual's birth. The astrology columns in newspapers, which are regularly read by 24 percent of the adult population, interpret the meaning of these forces for their readers and give them advice on how to best conduct their affairs.

The African primal world view also involves a belief in forces or powers which affect human behavior in important ways. For example, African primalists and many modern Africans firmly believe that the ancestors can help or hinder their progress in life; that the deities and spirits are able to cause sickness; that certain charms and magic, if properly prepared, will ensure that someone you love will return your love; and that it is possible for some people to see the future, for others to be transported instantly from one place to another, and for others to cause the death of someone without physically attacking them in any way. Like astrological forces, these forces are nonscientific in that they are not recognized as real by reputable modern physicists, chemists, or biologists. In contrast with astrology, however, these factors do not emanate from the planets. Africans believe instead that these forces reside in spiritual beings like the gods, spirits, and ancestors. Some of these beings are associated with natural objects such as lakes and hills, which thereby acquire a sacred character. They also believe that every living thing, including humans, has a life force and that the force of certain beings like kings may be as strong as or stronger than that of the spirits of lesser gods.

MANY FORCES

The world is seen as a multiplicity of spiritual forces by the traditional African. Some of these powers are spirits which may be encountered by the individual when deep in the heart of the forest, pulling a canoe along a particular bend in the river, at the height of noon as heat shimmers up from the packed red earth of the village square, or past midnight when everyone is asleep. The gods have powers which are regularly made manifest during their worship but which also may affect the lives of individuals without warning at any time. Right after death, as previously noted, the force of the dead is powerful and potentially dangerous. Later, if all goes well, the force becomes settled and, through ancestor worship, potentially available to the family in time of need.

If people have a king or chief, they are likely to believe that he is especially endowed with spiritual power which makes him immune to the magic of his enemies and dangerous to quarrel with. Other individuals who are regarded as sorcerers or witches also have this kind of power and are feared and treated with circumspection as a result. Among some peoples, individuals who are "unusual," like twins or albinos, are believed to be especially close to the gods and therefore to possess a higher than ordinary spiritual potency.

The preceding chapter examined the concept of the multiple self. Each of the four "souls" can be understood as a power or force. As described there, the transcendent-soul (Yoruba ori, or head) may affect the individual souls of other people. In a similar way, the individual-soul of the witch is believed to go out of the witch's body during sleep and to have the power to mystically "suck" the individual-souls of other people out of them so that they gradually decline and eventually die unless some remedial action is taken. The condition of a person's individual-soul is a measure of his or her personal potency. In the primal world view, therefore, sickness is seen as a diminution of the individual's potency, a weakening of the individual's mystical life power. Other adversities or afflictions such as not having children, lack of promotion at work, and even bad grades in school are also likely to be interpreted as a result of a weakening of the individual's vital potency.

INTERRELATIONSHIP OF FORCES

According to environmentalist Barry Commoner, one of the laws of ecology is that "everything is connected to everything else." This is true also for the spiritual ecology of African life. In the African primal world view, men or women are not viewed as autonomous individuals but as social beings whose life forces are, to quote the French student of African primal religions Placide Tempels, "in actual intimate and permanent rapport with other forces—a vital force both influenced by and influencing them."[1] This *mutual effect* that people have on each other is mystical. It is different from the influence people have on each other when they physically interact in work or at play. Perhaps the African concept of the interrelationship of forces can be better understood if it is thought of as an invisible field of force surrounding each person which interrelates with the fields of force of the other people with whom the person has contact, *as well* as with the forces associated with nature, the gods, and the ancestors. Because of this, if the well-being of one member of a family is threatened, in an important sense the collective well-being of the family is also threatened.

NATURE

As noted above, nature is also involved in the primal spiritual ecology. This is in striking contrast to the modern technological view of nature. To Africans, nature is "alive" in an important sense. Not only do animals have life forces, but many African peoples worship a god or goddess of the earth and/or the sky and believe that spirits are associated with certain trees, hills, lakes, and so on. As a result, the proper situation of humans in relation to nature is not exploitation or even conservation but *relationship.*

This relationship is not a passive reverence for life wherein humans treat all living things with an equal loving-kindness, as did St. Francis of Assisi and the famous missionary doctor Albert Schweitzer. As John Taylor points out, tribesmen in Africa are both as tender and as insensible in their treatment of other living things as people anywhere else. "There is often brutality in what they do, and in what they suffer, but always the relationship is essentially personal."[2] This personal relationship can be seen when a community hold its fertility festival to seek the blessing of gods to energize the crops and its thanksgiving festival to signify its gratitude for the gods' goodwill. It can also be seen when hunters make a brief sacrifice after killing a large animal in order to keep peace with its life force. In the traditional African world view humans are unique: they are able to harness forces for their benefit and

can legitimately sow the crops and reap the harvest and kill the wild beasts they need for food, but in doing so they must be accountable to the spiritual forces which are associated with these undertakings. It is truly a personalized universe that humans deal with and one which makes its demand on humans for sacrifices and the observance of taboos.

Chinua Achebe is a famous Nigerian novelist whose first novel about an Ibo village, *Things Fall Apart,* contains an episode which captures the close ties between humans and the earth and the collective responsibility which the whole community has for properly maintaining these ties. Okonkwo, the chief figure in the novel, is a hardworking and successful man, but one with a stubborn streak and a quick temper. To the horror of his neighbors he beat one of his wives in a rage during the annual Week of Peace in honor of the earth goddess Ani. That evening Ezeani, the priest of the earth goddess, called on Okonkwo and accused him of lacking respect for the people's gods and ancestors. In a stern voice he told him:

> You are not a stranger in Umuofia. You know as well as I do that our forefather ordained that before we plant any crops in the earth we should observe a week in which a man does not say a harsh word to his neighbor. We live in peace with our fellows to honor our great goddess of the earth without whose blessings our crops will not grow. You have committed a great evil. . . . The evil you have done can ruin the whole clan.[3]

A carving of the wife of Oduduwa, one of the Yoruba deities.

Okonkwo had to make a special sacrifice in order to try to placate the goddess.

BALANCE OF FORCES

A harmonious balance of forces is the ideal toward which traditional Africans strive. Okonkwo's intemperate action threatened the balance for his village, Umuofia, in a most serious manner, and only Ani's acceptance of his sacrifice would restore the situation and prevent inevitable misfortune. Often the creation of imbalance is not known until misfortune has actually occurred. This is because there are so many forces and so many chances to offend one force or the other unknowingly or unintentionally. The role of the diviner in these situations is all-important. He ascertains the source of imbalance among the complex of forces and what his client must do to set the balance straight again.

A number of African peoples appear to have what anthropologists call the "idea of the limited good." This is the notion that the amount of good or highly valued things is limited and that if one person suddenly has significantly more of something (such as a larger harvest) than usual, his or her good fortune could only be at the expense of neighbors and fellow villagers. For example, a Yoruba once told me how the richest man in his village was believed to have a special magic which mystically "sucked" the yams from his neighbors' fields to his own. His success was interpreted as being due to an unfair manipulation of powers and not to hard work or good luck. Neither misfortune nor exceptional fortune, but balance, is seen as the normal condition of human life.

HUMAN USE OF FORCES

Traditional Africans believe that human beings can use their creative intelligence and will to harness spiritual powers for their own use. This may be done by individuals or communities and it may be done to restore or to improve one's situation or to harm one's enemies. The selfish, antisocial use of spiritual force is hated and feared, whereas community-enhancing uses of spiritual force are welcomed and approved. To put it another way, there are legitimate and illegitimate uses of spiritual forces.

Before looking at some ways in which spiritual powers are harnessed, we need to consider the distinction between religion and magic. In Western culture religion and magic are often distinguished from each other in the following way. Magic is seen as the manipulation of spiritual power for human ends, whereas religion involves the worship of spiritual beings for their own sake. In magic the emphasis is on the proper form of the rite, whereas in religion it is on the intention of the worshipper. For the universal world religions like Islam and Christianity, such a distinction makes sense although there is often a fine line between magic and praying for victory in Saturday's game or seeking the intervention of a particular saint. In the primal religions, however, where the emphasis of the religions is this-worldly, the line between magic and religion is less distinct. Almost every ritual has its rules of performance, and many rituals are undertaken with a specific result in mind. The use of charms is widespread and regarded as normal. On the other hand, the gods and ancestors are viewed as having wills of their own, and their help for the individual is not automatic nor can it be compelled. It is further believed by many Africans that if a person is upright and good, he or she does not need to resort to protective magic. In other words, although many aspects of the primal religions are "magical" in the sense given above, the religions are much more than this and represent a genuine encounter between humans and the divine.

With this background in mind, let us now look at some of the many ways in which primalists seek to harness spiritual forces.

1. *By seeking knowledge of divine intentions through consulting diviners or oracles.* The role of the diviner-healer in African traditional cultures has already been described. Many of these cultures have several different religious practitioners who are believed to be able to ascertain divine intentions through one means or another. The diviners and oracles provide knowledge about the cause of misfortunes and/or a reading of the probable success of anticipated future ventures such as a long trip or the opening of a new business. This knowledge permits the individual to take the appropriate action, as described in the following items, to utilize spiritual forces.

2. *By approaching the ancestors and asking their intercession.* We have already seen how people approach the Egungun masqueraders during the Yoruba Egungun festival seeking intercession for their children. The Ndembu of northern Zambia have a class of ancestral-spirit rituals which are performed when individuals or groups have failed to honor their obligation to venerate the ancestors in some way and have been struck by misfortune as a result. The performance of these rituals seeks to restore the situation and to remove the ancestors' "curse."

3. *By approaching the gods and asking their intercession.* This may involve a positive appeal to the deity that the person or group worships or the performance of sacrificial rituals to redress the violation of a taboo associated with that deity or the neglect of some religious obligation owing to it.

4. *By employing the services of specialists in magic.* These individuals range from makers of charms to sorcerers. They are believed to have special esoteric knowledge of techniques that will harness spiritual power for particular needs. For example, an individual who feels threatened by witches may go to a charm maker and request a protective charm. The maker prepares some ingredients by a secret formula and places them inside a small leather pouch which is sewn up. The customer pays an agreed fee for the charm, which is then worn on his or her person. It is felt that the possession of the charm will convey protective spiritual power against the onslaughts of the witches. In Nigeria I once came upon a patch of cassava (a plant whose root is prepared and eaten) which an Ibo farmer had planted. The patch was some distance from his home and was far from any other dwelling. There was a vine strung around the entire patch, and attached to the vine in a conspicuous place was a charm. If thieves stole the ripe cassava before the farmer had a chance to harvest it himself, he believed that they would inevitably sicken and die as a result of the charm's power.

Sometimes people ask why traditional Africans continue to believe in spiritual powers and magic when charms fail to work or when sacrifices prescribed by a diviner fail to cure a sickness. The reason is that there is never a clear-cut, unambiguous failure and therefore it is always possible to rationalize a failure. Perhaps the diviner made a mistake. An individual who suspects that this is the case will simply consult another diviner, just as you or I might consult another doctor when we fail to recover from a sickness. Perhaps the client failed to observe the necessary taboos associated with the attempt to seek power. For example, when there was civil strife in Zaire (then the Congo) in the years immediately following independence in 1960, some rebel groups had religious practitioners who prepared magic which guaranteed that the enemy's bullets would turn into water. Associated with the success of the magic was the observance of a taboo against sexual intercourse immediately before the battle and an injunction not to turn one's head away from the battle. When someone was struck and killed by a "nonliquid" bullet (as often happened), it was easy enough for his comrades in arms to blame it on his violation of one of the taboos rather than on the inefficacy of the magic itself.

Finally, perhaps the enemy or the witch simply had greater power than the charm. Then the individual would need to obtain a more powerful charm.

Chapter 7

Evil

What causes sickness, suffering, and death? In particular, what causes apparently undeserved misfortune? Why do some good people prosper in life while other equally good people suffer? These are fundamental questions of meaning which all religions try to answer. Some religions answer the question by denying the importance or even the fundamental reality of earthly life. Of the religions that accept the reality of earthly existence, some more or less beg the question by appealing to God's inscrutable will while others posit an evil force as the ultimate source of human misery. In the case of the African primal religions, they are this-worldly, and their ultimate explanation of evil is that it is the work of witches and sorcerers.

THE LOGIC OF CAUSATION

In the African primal world view, most events are not believed to happen by chance, especially if they involve "unnatural" misfortune. Whether a particular event is viewed as natural or unnatural is, of course, relative. What is natural to one person may be unnatural to someone else. In traditional African society, certain misfortunes like the death of a newborn baby are, unfortunately, viewed as natural because of the very high infant death rate. On the other hand, the death of children once they are weaned, or of adults, is not viewed as natural; nor, as already noted, are the deaths of a series of infants to the same mother. In cases like these—or in cases of serious accidental injury, sickness, inability to have children, or serious crop failure—a search for the cause of the event will most likely be undertaken. This will happen even when the immediate cause, like a tree falling on a young man who is cutting it down, is known. The search will seek to answer the question of why the tree happened to fall on *that* young man. Put another way, the question is, *who* caused the tree to fall on that young man? This is a search for mystical, rather than physical, causation. In the case cited above, it is decidedly not a search for the person who actually cut the tree down. Instead it is a search for the spiritual force which may have worked on the young man's mind to distract him, thereby causing him to be careless.

There are a number of different mystical forces which may be blamed for misfortunes like this one. These may be divided into three categories:

1. Forces which are activated by human mistakes and failures.
2. Forces which represent arbitrary chance.
3. Forces which are fundamentally evil and malicious.

FORCES ACTIVATED BY HUMAN MISTAKES AND FAILURES

Traditional African life in close-knit communities involves people in numerous obligations toward one another and toward the ancestors, gods, and spirits. These obligations are sanctified by tradition. For example, the child owes respect to his other parents, the younger brother to the older brother, the ordinary person to the chief, the junior wife to the senior wife, the son to the deceased father, the worshipper of a particular deity to that deity, and so on. When these obligations are fulfilled and the forces are in balance, a community is healthy. If an obligation is not fulfilled, either through deliberate neglect or insult or through a simple act of forgetfulness, a possible cause of misfortune is created. The offended party may manipulate mystical forces through magic, as in the case of a person laying a curse on a kinsman, or may use inherent power, as in the case of an ancestrally caused sickness. Generally these misfortunes are individual, but sometimes the violation of a taboo, such as Okonkwo's angry outburst during the annual Week of Peace, will threaten an entire community.

It is the job of the diviner-healer to locate the source of the misfortune and to identify the failure which needs to be rectified. For example, an individual was born into a family group which traditionally worshipped a particular deity. His own participation in the cult of that deity, like that of a number of other people in his family, was very sporadic. When he was struck down by a persistent illness that did not respond to ordinary treatment, he consulted a diviner-healer who told him that the deity was angry with him and that only if he performed some special sacrifices and participated actively in the deity's cult would he be cured of his illness. Sometimes the services of the diviner-healer are not required, as in the case of pregnant women who have an unusually prolonged labor. It is widely believed that one cause of this condition is adulterous behavior on a woman's part. She is urged to confess her immoral behavior and to name the man involved. Stories are told of women whose labor ended quickly and easily once they made their confession.

Neglecting the ancestors, insulting senior people, failing to observe certain taboos, or committing immoral acts may therefore all result in some sort of "deserved" misfortune. Since the number of obligations is very large and since people are always guilty of some breach of conduct or another, the potential causes of misfortune are ever present. When this kind of cause is identified, it is believed that recompense in the form of sacrifices and possibly participation in certain public religious rituals will restore the injured relationship and lead to an end of the misfortune.

FORCES WHICH REPRESENT ARBITRARY CHANCE

Some African peoples number among their divinities one which is especially associated with misfortune and the uncertainties which mark daily life. The Yoruba god Eshu is such a divinity. Basically Eshu is the trickster deity. He has a great deal of power and is highly respected. Some say that he is a messenger of the gods; others say that even the Supreme Being is subordinate to Eshu in certain matters. Eshu's character is such that his "hobby" is creating mischief. He likes to spoil things for no reason. Although he is a source of evil, he is definitely not evil incarnate. If someone is on Eshu's good side, it is believed that Eshu will protect that person. Thus it is common to see mounds of earth in front of many Yoruba houses where simple offerings are made to Eshu. Carvings of Eshu typically portray him as an impish fellow playing a Yoruba flute.

When the Christian missionaries were translating their religious literature into African languages, they searched for a word which meant "devil" in these languages. Invariably they had difficulties because the primal world view does not include a single deity which embodies the principle of evil in this way. Sometimes they did not realize this and mistakenly called the trickster divinity the devil. As one can see, there is a great deal of difference between the Yoruba's flute-playing Eshu and the pitchfork-wielding devil of Christian mythology whose aim is to tempt humans to an afterlife of eternal damnation.

FORCES WHICH ARE FUNDAMENTALLY EVIL AND MALICIOUS

The closest thing in African cultures to sources of fundamental evil are sorcerers and witches. Whereas Africans believe that all humans and even all the divinities (especially the trickster divinity) act in a malicious way at times, true sorcerers and witches are *always* malicious. They cause sickness and death in their victims for no valid reason; they are believed to act out of pure, unjustified malice.

Africans believe that the basic difference between sorcerers and witches is the way in which they harness mystical powers to achieve their evil ends and the intention they have toward their victims. *Sorcerers* have to manipulate material objects and perform rituals in order to harm their victims, whereas *witches* simply use their innate power to accomplish the same end. Sorcerers always deliberately intend to harm their victims, whereas witches do not always consciously realize the harm that they cause—their power is to some extent beyond their personal control. It is not true that sorcerers are always men and witches women, although this tends to be the case.

Having distinguished the two types of evildoer, it is important to point out that there is the usual variation among African cultures in the importance attributed to witchcraft and sorcery. Virtually all African peoples believe in one or the other of these evildoers; and many, like the Zande or the Yoruba, clearly distinguish the two types and believe in both. Others may believe in only one or the other of them, like the Lele who live in southwest Zaire and who have strong beliefs in sorcery but none in witchcraft.

Sorcery

Sorcerers are people who have the ability to work harmful magic against others. They do this in much the same way that healers work curative magic, using various materials, actions, and a formula of words in a ritual. Typically when sorcery is worked against a particular person, the sorcerer needs to have some contact with the intended victim through his or her nail clippings or a lock of hair or even with the scraped-up dust of the person's footprints. Sorcery is for hire, and people who have enemies or rivals can pay for expert sorcerers to perform the necessary harmful magic. It is also possible for people to learn some sorcery and do it themselves. When sorcery is used in this way, the motives which lie behind the harm done to the victim are understandable, however much they may be condemned. Indeed, recourse to sorcery by someone who was injured by another person

66

may be justified, and sorcery in this sense does not fall into the category of fundamental evil. Among some peoples the diviner-healers also have the capacity to work retaliative magic.

When sorcery is performed by someone whose *only* specialty is harmful magic, however, that person is deeply feared and hated. And the sorcerer who is fully committed to doing evil acts for their own sake creates the presence of pure evil. Mary Douglas, who has studied the beliefs of the Lele people in Zaire, says that they think that anyone with a powerful motive might commit sorcery once or twice but that "the person whom the Lele feared and abhorred was the fully committed sorcerer, given over entirely to his lusts." They believe that the victims of such a person turn into animals that obey his wishes but crave human flesh which he has to provide for them in the form of new victims.

> In this way the Lele saw the once-committed sorcerer pressed on to kill more and more. He became utterly depraved, denatured. He had broken kinship with mankind, and made it with the wild beasts. . . . While he existed in a village no enterprise could prosper. For jealousy of their happiness he killed small children.[1]

Witchcraft

The witch is an individual who is believed to have an inherent power to harm other people and an addiction to doing so. Witches perform their evil deeds at night. Many African peoples believe that witches use "familiars," or animals which may at times take the form of human beings. Often witches are thought to belong to societies of witches which meet at night to eat human souls. An individual may deliberately join the society of witches, or an individual may inherit the power or even acquire it involuntarily. For example, there is a strong belief among the Xhosa in South Africa that witch familiars which are sometimes "ownerless" manage to attach themselves to an innocent person who then becomes a witch without realizing it.

The details of beliefs in witchcraft vary among African peoples, but the fundamental reality is very similar. To the African, witchcraft has a nightmare quality about it. Anyone can be a victim, often for no reason. Witches may and often do kill their close kin. It is even believed that some mothers sacrifice their children to the witch society. In a sense, therefore, witches form an antisociety which glorifies the opposite of what the normal society believes in. Horrible as this antisociety may be, however, Africans realize that witches are still a part of their community. Thus there is an ambivalence about witches and a belief among many peoples that witches can be reintegrated into the community if they confess and if certain rituals are performed. Nowhere is this ambivalence better expressed than in one of the names the Yoruba use to refer indirectly to the witches. (To refer to witches directly is thought to be bad luck since they might hear you and take an interest in you.) This name is *awon iya,* which means "our mothers." Women are the source of life, and yet witches among the Yoruba are always women; so, ironically, women are also the source of undeserved death!

If someone is suspected of being a witch—and often older women who have few kin and live on the margin of social relationships acquire this reputation—people treat them with care, not wanting to provoke them. But since anybody can be a witch, sometimes without knowing it, it is not surprising that when senseless misfortune strikes or when normal remedies and sacrifices fail to cure a persistent sickness, accusations of witchcraft are made. In a close-knit society where people live in a small village and have to deal with each other daily, such accusations usually cause intense animosity and conflict. In some societies the accusations may only be made covertly, however, and the victims will defend themselves by obtaining the advice of diviner-healers or other religious specialists as to what antiwitchcraft sacrifices and rituals they need to perform to ward off the witch's evil power. In other societies, however, the accusations may be made publicly. In these societies the poison ordeal may be used to determine the truth of these accusations. Typically, both the person accused and the accuser drink the poison which is ritually administered by a priest. If the poison is vomited, the person lives and is believed to be innocent. If it is not, the poison causes a sure and agonizing death. Arbitrary and cruel as such an ordeal may seem, it does serve to clear the air of accusations by providing a generally accepted measure of guilt or innocence.

WITCHCRAFT AMONG THE BADYARANKE

Let us take a look at witchcraft among a single African people, the Badyaranke of Senegal. For many months, William Simmons, an American anthropologist, lived in the small Badyaranke village of Tonghia; and his book, *Eyes of the Night,* describes their way of life. The account that follows is based on his study.[2]

The Badyaranke believe that most sicknesses, accidents, and deaths are caused by witches. The witch captures and eats his or her victim's soul in an invisible way. Witches are members of a society of witches. After a witch has killed someone, the witch invites the other witches to join in the feast. By attending the feast, each guest acquires an obligation to return the favor. Debts are increased with each kill and thus the threat of killings by witches never ends.

On the second night that Simmons spent in Tonghia, the quiet of the night and his sleep were suddenly interrupted by a loud gunshot as his host's son shot at a large owl that had settled in a nearby tree. It was months later that Simmons learned the real meaning of this event. It seems that a witch who has hosted a feast is believed to arrive in the debtor's village in the guise of a bird. The bird then cries like an owl to announce its impatience for a soul. An owl had begun to cry near the hut where Simmons slept, and the gunshot was meant to drive the witch away before any misfortune could happen.

The Badyaranke believe that witches can transform themselves freely into various kinds of animals, even into a breeze. They travel about at will. The witches kill with invisible guns, ropes, clubs, knives, and poisons. They are organized into a society which, like the ordinary human society, has chiefs. Anyone, male or female, can become a witch. The powers are said to be transmitted through heredity. In the past, people told Simmons, only old people were witches. Even today, however, elderly female witches are still thought to be especially numerous and very powerful.

Africans say that witches tend to choose their victims by two criteria: (1) whether the victim's death is likely to raise a threat of reprisal and (2) whether the witch has anger for the person. This is why witch killings are believed to take place within families so often. The Badyaranke believe that blood relatives would be less likely to seek vengeance. Simmons reports that a male witch would not care to kill his wife, however, because it would be costly and difficult to replace her. It is believed that witches are most likely to attack people in the village at night and during the period of the rice harvest. Rice harvesttime is when the strong young men are gone and the village is quiet and partially abandoned. Although the choice of victims is somewhat predictable and anger does figure in that choice, it is believed that most witches kill not because of anger but because of being caught up in reciprocal obligations with other witches. This is because if a witch does not provide victims for his or her former hosts, the witch is liable to be eaten instead.

Because of the widespread belief in the activities of the witches, the people use a wide variety of charms and other techniques to protect themselves from their power. For example, women who have borne a series of children who have died in infancy may give a surviving child an unattractive name in order to make the child less appealing to a witch who might wish to take the child away. Thus some children are given names such as Feces or No-name. Other people, such as the Yoruba, have secret societies whose basic function is either to "fight" the witches (the Oro Society) or to keep on their good side (the Gelede Society). It is widely believed in different parts of Africa that an important role of the ancestors is to protect the living from the horrible acts of the witches.

Given the existence of the witches and their powers of the night, it also becomes imperative for the Badyaranke to have ways of learning whether a particular death was caused by witchcraft and of identifying witches. Simmons learned that there are several different techniques. One of these is to hire one of the two Muslim priests in the area who are famous for their ability to identify witches. It is said that these men actually identify specific witches and have a technique for removing their powers by making a small cut under each of the alleged witches' eyes, for which they charge a large fee. The other favored technique is recourse to one of at least six oracular techniques for obtaining information about witches. In the past the Badyaranke used the poison oracle to determine the truth of a witchcraft accusation, but in present-day Senegal this technique is no longer permitted. Among the contemporary oracular techniques is the hot-iron ordeal. Someone who is accused may ask the blacksmith to heat a piece of iron until it is red hot and then to place it in a nest of leaves held in the accused's cupped hands. If the hands are burned, the person is assumed to be guilty.

Although the Badyaranke claim that convicted witches were previously killed, Simmons doubts that this was the case. Instead, ostracism and possibly exile were the ultimate sanctions for witches who failed to confess and be "de-witched."

In common with a number of other anthropologists who have studied the world view of traditional Africans, Simmons finds that in many ways the witches and their society are an *inversion* of normal Badyaranke society. Witches are invisible and live by night. They turn into animals, walk upside down, cause families to break up, kill next of kin, and have an insatiable need to kill. "Men and women work to create and sustain life; witches work to release it, to exploit the hard-won social and cultural order for their own ends. . . . They defy physical constraints, they contradict basic categories and they act in ways that men should not act."[3]

THE REALITY OF WITCHCRAFT

In traditional Africa no one questions the fact that witches really exist. Children learn about witches at an early age. They hear their parents refer to them indirectly; they see the fear in people's faces when certain people are mentioned; and they see people suffer from sickness and, at times, die for no discernible cause other than witchcraft. Finally, they will have heard of, or may even have personally listened to, an accused witch confess to his or her witchcraft.

How would such occurrences be explained by someone from a Western culture? The following might be a typical explanation. Humans do not have an innate power to harm others through witchcraft. Instead, the "power" of witchcraft in African societies comes from four factors. First, serious sickness and death are far more common in traditional societies than they are in Western society. Literally one out of every two children dies before the age of five! Second, these traditional societies do not have an understanding of the scientific cause of illness. Therefore, like our ancestors, they think it is highly plausible that mystical forces may be involved. Third, they live in societies where *everybody* shares the belief in witchcraft. In a situation of uncertainty, social psychologists have shown that people are strongly influenced by the beliefs of others. You yourself probably know how hard it is to go against the opinion of your crowd. After living in Nigeria for some months among people who believed in evil powers, I myself could feel the power of those widespread beliefs working against my belief that a combination of chance and natural forces causes sickness and death. Fourth, these Africans live in societies that are close-knit, where people in small villages have to live and work together even though they may sometimes dislike each other or harbor jealousies. The polygamous family where a husband has several wives is common in African societies and is a potential source of strains and jealousies.

In societies charactized by these four factors, witchcraft makes a certain amount of sense in that it provides an answer for events that demand some kind of explanation. The explanation is "logical" to the people because they in fact harbor hatreds toward other people at times; and thus when someone becomes mysteriously sick and dies, it makes sense to them to think that a person who harbored a grudge against him or her may have caused that sickness. The confessions that alleged witches sometimes make can be understood as the effect of a guilty conscience. Consider a situation in which a woman is jealous of one of her co-wives. She may even dream of hurting the woman; for Africans, as for many prescientific peoples, dreams are thought to be, in a sense, real. Then one of this co-wife's children dies. Suspicion turns toward the woman. Is it surprising if, under the circumstances, she confesses that she must be a witch and has used her power to kill the child?

Chapter 8

Dying But Very Much Alive

Until this chapter we have been discussing traditional African culture. For the last one thousand years, however, Islam has been slowly spreading into black Africa, and in the past one hundred years both Muslims and Christians have been working hard and with great success to convert Africans from primal religions to their universal religions. How have these efforts affected the primal religions? Are the African primal religions still strong today? What is the future of the primal religions?

The answer to these questions is summarized in a paradox: the primal religions are dying but are still very much alive. Although they are rapidly being supplanted as institutional religions by Islam and Christianity, the primal world view continues to be a very important part of the world view of many Africans who today recognize Allah or the Christian God as the object of their belief and religious allegiance. In this way African primal religions continue to be a living force which must be appreciated if contemporary African culture is to be understood.

RAPID CHANGE

The twentieth-century advance of Islam and Christianity in Africa has resulted in one of the most massive religious transformations in the history of the world. Probably more than fifty million Africans have already changed their basic religious allegiance in this period as adherents of African primal religions are more and more turning from their former faith to either of these two universal world religions. By the year 2000, the communal institutional expressions of African primal religion will be few indeed, and probably only a handful of peoples living in very remote areas will continue to practice a primal religion as a living communal religion.

Why have the primal religions been so vulnerable to Islam and Christianity? The answer to this question lies in the local character of the primal religions. As long as traditional African societies are relatively isolated and untouched by rapid change and modernization, their religions provide a satisfactory and unchallenged interpretation of the meaning of life. But when African peoples are exposed to other groups on a regular basis, as happened to those groups that were touched by the trans-Saharan trade in past centuries and to all of the groups once colonial rule was imposed, Islam and Christianity become increasingly attractive. They both proclaim a God that is the God of all peoples, and such a universal deity makes sense of the new diversity of life. More than this, the Muslims and Christians who worship such a God in other lands also have a more technologically advanced culture. This was true of both the Muslim traders who crossed the Sahara from North Africa and the Christian missionaries. Although compared to Europe of the nineteenth century the North African Muslim societies were less technologically advanced, they had great cities, writing, books, scholars, and a more advanced technology than the African tribal societies. Thus the two new religions, which of course were both religions of "the Book," are attractive to people undergoing change because they are viewed as modern.

When they first are introduced into a community, Islam and, to a lesser extent, Christianity sometimes assimilate aspects of primal religion and/or tolerate certain primal practices and beliefs such as divination and healing. But these aspects are subordinated to the overall religious framework of the universal religions and are removed from their place in the former totality of the primal religion. Direct worship of the primal deities is never tolerated. As a consequence of the spread of Islam and Christianity, cults of the primal deities die out, the communal festivals lose their significance even if they continue to exist, the secret societies lose their attraction, and rites of passage either die out or are transformed into Christian or Muslim rites. Most important of all is the fact that the unity of the primal religions as communal religions becomes disturbed. The old sanctity of custom is undermined. They are now just one of several religions instead of being *the* religion.

African primal religions are not alone in being vulnerable to the spread of universal world religions. Primal religions in other parts of the world have also declined in a similar fashion, as among the peoples of Melanesia and Polynesia in the face of Christian missionizing. It is interesting to note, however, that wherever Christian missionaries have tried to convert peoples who were already adherents of one of the other universal world religions, such as the Hindus and Muslims of India or the followers of Confucius in China, the Christian converts have been very few. Unlike the primal religions in Africa, the universal religions in these communities continue to provide their adherents with sufficient resources to cope with even the rapid changes brought about by the spread of modernization and industrialization.

THE SPREAD OF ISLAM

How did Islam spread into black Africa? Soon after the death of the Prophet Muhammad in A.D. 632, there was some contact between Islam and black Africa; but Islam did not come in full tide until the eleventh century when Ibn Yasin, a Muslim missionary of Sufi mystical persuasion, established himself among the Berbers in present-day Mauritania. His followers, a Sufi order known as the Almoravids, created a vast empire and influenced powerful neighboring tribal chiefs through peaceful and military means. Thus for the first time black Africans were converted to Islam. This was an era when great black African empires such as Mali and Ghana rose and fell in the vast Sahel region of West Africa, a dry land of the edge of the Sahara traversed by the great Niger River which meanders on its way to the ocean a thousand miles away.

As early as 1050, the ruling monarch of the ancient Mali Empire was a Muslim. The diffusion of Islam to the common people was very slow, however, and its spread through the interior of northern West Africa took many centuries. It is only in the last century, since colonialism, that the peoples in the rain forest along the coast have begun to accept Islam.

In East Africa the advance of Islam took place in quite a different manner. The map on page 76 shows how, in West Africa, Islam spread from the interior toward the coast, whereas in East Africa it spread in two different ways. The first of these is shown by arrow A. Since the seventh century, Islamicized tribes have carried their religion down the Nile Valley, ultimately resulting in the strongly Islamic culture of the northern half of the Sudan. Primal religions are still strong in the southern part of that country, however. Attempts were made by Muslim armies over the centuries to conquer the Christian kingdom of Aksum (an ancient kingdom in what is now Ethiopia). But aided by its inaccessible mountains, the kingdom was able to repel the invaders successfully.

Arrows B and C depict the contacts made by Arab traders and groups of immigrant Arab Muslims along the East African coast. Although these contacts began as early as the seventh century, their impact on the black African populations of the interior has been much less compared with the spread of Islam in West Africa. This is because none of these Arab Muslim communities pursued an active policy of trying

SPREAD OF ISLAM

to convert their African neighbors. They remained insulated from their surroundings and always looked to the Arabian Peninsula as "home." To be sure, some East Africans became Muslims over the centuries, and a coastal culture developed with mixed African and Arab elements. One result of this culture is Swahili, a lingua franca (common language) now widely spoken in East Africa. It is basically a Bantu (African linguistic family) language with many Arabic words in its vocabulary. After the colonial takeover at the end of the last century, Islam began to accelerate its advance in both East and West Africa.

THE SPREAD OF CHRISTIANITY

The first contact between Christianity and black Africans occurred three hundred years before Muhammad's birth. After the conversion in A.D. 324 of Emperor Azana, king of Aksum, to a form of Orthodox Christianity, the resulting Ethiopian Orthodox Church remained isolated in the Ethiopian highlands. Although the Christian kingdom was periodically beleaguered by Muslim armies, the Ethiopian Orthodox Church has survived until the present. The second attempt to spread Christianity in black Africa was not successful, however. It was begun by the Catholic kingdom of Portugal in the fifteenth century and continued for the next several hundred years. Portugal, as a result of the pioneering exploratory voyages made by a series of daring sea captains under the sponsorship of Prince Henry "the Navigator," eventually circumnavigated Africa and in the process established trading and diplomatic relations with a number of African coastal peoples. Roman Catholic missionaries were sent to these peoples and achieved some initial success in converting them to Christianity.

One of the most notable temporary Roman Catholic successes was the Christian conversion of Afonso, king of the Kongo people (who live in present-day Zaire, Congo, and Angola), shortly after A.D. 1500 and in the continuance of Catholic influence among the Kongo for over 150 years. Across the continent Portuguese Jesuits pushed their way inland from the mouth of the Zambesi River into what is now Rhodesia. Their first missionary priest was martyred in 1561, some 600 miles from the mouth of the Zambesi, but in 1652 a paramount chief in the area was baptized by the Dominicans.

In the end, however, the primal religions of the peoples touched by the Portuguese held firm, as the character of the Portuguese contact degenerated into exploitation. By 1800, essentially all that remained of this attempt to spread Catholic Christianity were the smoldering remains of a few stone chapels in what is now Angola and Mozambique and some crucifixes and other Christian religious objects which found their way into the court religious paraphernalia of the firmly "pagan" rulers.

If these first two attempts to establish Christianity in black Africa met with mixed results, the third attempt, in the modern era, has been a stunning success. At the end of the eighteenth century a concern to convert the "heathen" populations of the world to Christianity began to be articulated among Protestant Christians and resulted in the modern missionary movement. Africa quickly became the object of a considerable missionary activity in which Catholic missionaries were soon heavily involved. All up and down the coast from the 1800's onward, missionaries from Portugal and other European countries as well as the United States made their first contacts with coastal peoples. As soon as possible they pushed inland from their coastal bases to reach the interior peoples. By 1880, a number of mission stations had been established throughout the continent. These served as centers for both conversion to Christianity and for the spread of the European way of life.

In this initial phase (1800–1885) of the Christian missionary impact on Africa, the number of converts was relatively small. The missionaries were hampered by disease, unstable political conditions in some parts of Africa, and the resistance of the practitioners and believers of the primal religions themselves. By 1885, however, the stage was set for the rapid increase in Christianity which subsequently ensued. Medical progress now made it possible to treat malaria and guarantee a reasonable life expectancy for missionaries. Many African languages had been reduced to writing by the missionaries so that the new converts could read the Christian Bible in their own tongue. The first missionary schools had been established where Christian and non-Christian youth could learn about religion and be prepared to participate in the modern way of life, and these schools were very successful in influencing many of the future leaders of the African countries to become Christians.

Of greatest importance for the advance of Christianity, however, was the colonial takeover of Africa which began at this time and was completed by the end of World War I. Before this time, the missionaries had often advanced into the interior far beyond the influence of the European nations. Now the colonial rule of the British, the French, the Belgians, the Germans, and the Portuguese brought tribal wars to an end, improved communications, and fostered a modern way of life based on a literate culture, a money economy, and linkage to the rest of the world. The colonial rulers were sympathetic to the work of the missionaries on the whole and subsidized the mission schools, which expanded rapidly. Christianity was seen by many Africans as the religion of the powerful conqueror and found popularity among people who viewed it as the wave of the future.

It should be noted that the expansion of colonial rule at this time also fostered the expansion of Islam in areas where Islam already had a presence. Islam, while not the religion of the conqueror, was nevertheless also viewed by many as offering a satisfactory way of coming to terms with change. Africans viewed both Christianity and Islam as "civilized" religions. The primal religions, on the other hand, were viewed as too local and unsophisticated to be able to continue institutionally in the new "modern" world that was rapidly developing.

THE PRESENT SITUATION

The latest comprehensive data[1] showing the religious allegiance of black Africans are for 1972. These are *not* actual membership figures, but they represent estimates of the number of people who would tell someone like a census taker that they "belong" to a particular religion. The data, which include every independent black African country (but not South Africa, South-West Africa, and Rhodesia), give the following distribution:

Adherents of primal religions	65,000,000	21%
Muslims	116,000,000	37%
Christians	131,000,000	42% /

Compare this with the situation one hundred years previous to this time when probably 75 to 80 percent of the Africans in this part of Africa were primalists. It is difficult to know the magnitude of the changes since 1972, but there is no doubt that the change toward Islam and Christianity has continued to be rapid. Nevertheless, it can reasonably be assumed that today at least a fifth of black Africans continue to be firmly identified with the primal religions. In terms of sheer numbers, therefore, there are far more adherents of the primal-type religions in Africa today than anywhere else in the world.

The map on page 80 shows how the adherents of the various religions are distributed throughout the continent. The eight countries which have 50 percent or more of their populations as adherents of primal religions are indicated by an asterisk. They comprise two clusters: one in West Africa and one in Central Africa. The special reasons for the persistence of primal religions in these countries is not known, but it probably has to do with a combination of (1) the relative lack of contact with modernizing forces, (2) the presence of a decentralized ("stateless") traditional political system, and (3) the relative lack of sustained contact with missionaries.

ISLAM AND CHRISTIANITY
IN CONTEMPORARY AFRICA

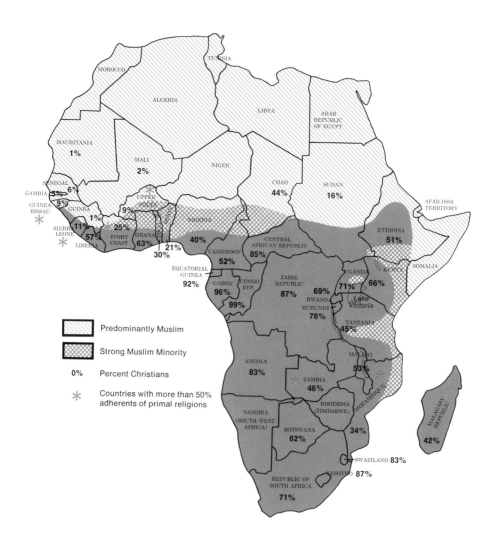

TUNISIA

MOROCCO

ALGERIA

LIBYA

ARAB
REPUBLIC
OF EGYPT

MAURITANIA
1%

MALI
2%

NIGER

CHAD
44%

SUDAN
16%

AFAR-ISSA
TERRITORY

SENEGAL
6%

GAMBIA **5%**

GUINEA
BISSAU **9%**

GUINEA
1%

UPPER
VOLTA **9%**

NIGERIA

CENTRAL
AFRICAN REPUBLIC
85%

ETHIOPIA
51%

SIERRA
LEONE **11%**

57%

LIBERIA

IVORY
COAST **63%**

GHANA

21%
30%

40%

CAMEROON
52%

SOMALIA

EQUATORIAL
GUINEA
92%

GABON
96%

CONGO
REP.

99%

ZAIRE
REPUBLIC
87%

RWANDA

BURUNDI
76%

UGANDA
69%

71%

KENYA
66%

Lake
Victoria

TANZANIA
45%

ANGOLA
83%

ZAMBIA
46%

MALAWI
53%

NAMIBIA
(SOUTH-WEST
AFRICA)

RHODESIA
(ZIMBABWE)

MOZAMBIQUE

MALAGASY
REPUBLIC
42%

BOTSWANA
62%

34%

SWAZILAND **83%**

REPUBLIC OF
SOUTH AFRICA
71%

LESOTHO **87%**

Predominantly Muslim

Strong Muslim Minority

0%   Percent Christians

*   Countries with more than 50%
adherents of primal religions

BUT VERY MUCH ALIVE

If the estimate of 21 percent for the present number of adherents of the primal religions is correct, at least sixty million black Africans still live in something approximating the full communal institutional context of these religions. Since it is "fashionable" in many parts of Africa today to publicly count oneself as a Muslim or Christian, there are doubtless many more millions of Africans who are in reality far more involved in the primal religions than in their professed Muslim or Christian faith. Thus the primal religions are still very much alive, at least for the present.

But there is another, more important sense in which the primal religions continue as living religious influences. As indicated at the beginning of this chapter, if we are to really grasp the present importance of primal religion, we have to look beyond the institutional expression of the religion and consider the persistence of primal world view. This persistence is considerable among many, many Africans who are actually practicing Muslims or Christians, even including those who are highly educated.

Once very recently when I was in Washington, D.C., I took a taxi and discovered that my taxi driver was a Yoruba from Nigeria. I told him that I had spent several years in Ibadan, and we had an enjoyable talk about my work in Nigeria and his life in America. It turned out that he had been in the United States for five years studying for a B.A. and now for an M.A. at Howard University in Washington and was driving the taxi to help with his expenses. He was a second-generation Christian and had gone to a grade school and high school run by the Nigerian Anglican Church. He also told me that he had recently been suffering from a debilitating illness which resisted every kind of medical treatment he tried. After consulting with his family in Nigeria, he had reached the conclusion that the cause of the sickness was the spirit of his father who had died several years before!

Why would the spirit of the father affect the son? From our analysis of the primal world view in the previous chapters, the logic of this belief should not surprise you. The dead are owed respect and have power over the living according to primal African belief. Traditionally, Yoruba have several funeral ceremonies for a dead person. The first of these is held immediately after death. The second, which is really a service of commemoration, occurs after a year or so has passed. Through these rituals the spirit of the dead person is put to rest. If the rituals are properly performed, the spirit of the dead father will bring good luck and fortune to the family and, of course, if they are not properly performed, the opposite may be the result.

Today the Nigerian Christian churches have Christian funeral services and they also have a Christian version of the second service, too. My driver, as the eldest son, had a special responsibility for seeing that the performance of his second ceremony took place, but it had been delayed because of his absence from the country. He believed that this delay had angered his father's spirit. He therefore gave directions for the ceremony to be performed and sent a large money contribution to his family to help cover the expenses of the lavish entertaining which the modern version of the ceremony requires. He told me that he now felt a good deal better and attributed his cure to the ritual action he had initiated.

This example shows how strong the traditional world view is, even among educated Christians. Christianity has always been more severe in its condemnation of every aspect of the primal religions than Islam, and, indeed, many missionaries blindly condemned the whole traditional way of life of African peoples. Education and residence away from the village tend to weaken the bonds of the primal world view. Thus, if a well-educated African Christian such as the taxi driver is so involved with the primal world view in this way (and he is not an isolated exception), the extent of its continued influence in contemporary Africa can well be imagined.

This is why the traditional diviner-healers have continued to thrive even in the large cities, although they now have many "modern" African competitors who offer such things as astrological counseling, Western occult techniques, and patent medicines for surefire cures. These practitioners are consulted by workers desiring a promotion, men seeking to win a woman's love, people suffering from malaria or any one of a number of other diseases which remain untreated because of the great shortage of doctors and modern medical facilities, and even by political leaders such as former president of Ghana, Kwame Nkrumah, who was reputed to consult a renowned diviner in Guinea during times of political uncertainty.

But while there is continuity, there is also change. The religious beliefs of my Yoruba taxi driver are very different from those of non-Christian primalists. He has made a crucial break with his traditional religious heritage, and while he draws on certain aspects of it, it is transformed and dominated by his Christian beliefs. He would never think of worshipping the old deities; he would never join a traditional secret society; he views the Egungun masqueraders roughly as many Catholics view the saints; and for him the annual festival which commemorates his city's major deity is essentially a patriotic rather than religious occasion. But supernatural power, magic, and witchcraft are realities to him, and in times of stress he does not think it wrong to consult a traditional diviner-healer for divination. Other Africans have developed a new form of Christianity which provides a distinctly Christian way of handling these problems without recourse to either the old or the new practitioners. These prophet-healing churches and the future of the traditional world view will be discussed in the next chapter.

Chapter 9

Prophet-Healing Religion

One of the most interesting aspects of the spread of Christianity among African peoples has been the spontaneous emergence of a genuinely *African* form of Christianity in the form of prophet-healing churches. The first of these churches appeared in South Africa and Nigeria some sixty years ago. Today almost every African tribe which has had a large number of people converted to Christianity, especially Protestant Christianity, has its share of these churches. In 1968 it was estimated that there were over five thousand independent churches, as they are sometimes called, with some seven million adherents and that they were increasing rapidly. Probably one out of every twelve African Christians is affiliated with a prophet-healing church.[1]

The founders and leaders of the prophet-healing churches are called prophets. These prophets are typically Christians who claim to have received a vision from God which empowered them to heal in his name. Sometimes they try to stay within the mission church at first, but as they gather followers and develop a set of practices which differ from those of the parent church (such as permitting polygyny or requiring their followers not to use any form of medicine), they tend to separate and establish their own church.

Africa today is a unique blend of traditional and modern elements, as shown by this Ibo herbal doctor (top) and an Anglican church service in Sierra Leone.

THEIR CAUSE

These churches are a significant response to the unsettling effects of rapid religious change in Africa. They arose primarily because of the failure of the missionaries to relate Christianity to the African traditional world view. As was pointed out in the last chapter, the missionaries often made the mistake of blindly condemning the traditional way of life. Theirs was an English or an American version of Christianity which, in certain respects, required their converts to transform themselves culturally into black Englishmen or Americans. For example, until relatively recently, African Christians had to be baptized with "Christian" first names such as Paul or Silas. An African name which might mean "God is with me" was unacceptable because it was African!

A crucial example of the clash between the missionary form of Christianity and the traditional world view came from the missionaries' emphasis on life after death. As previously noted, the traditional world view emphasized life in this world, and much of traditional religion involved protection against witches and sorcerers as well as healing. The missionaries, however, tended to ignore the reality of these evil beings for their African converts. They did not recognize that sickness was still a deeply religious problem for their new converts. Instead of offering "protection" against these evil powers through prayer and fasting, therefore, they tended to urge their converts to have faith and to look forward to their reward in the afterlife. They forgot that in such past times as the Middle Ages, to say nothing of Palestine at the time of Christ, Christianity took the presence of evil powers for granted and offered believers power and protection against them. Of course, some converts were able to make this cultural jump from the traditional world view to the modern Western world view, but many others found it very difficult. It is not surprising that some of these people would go to church on Sunday and then quietly consult a traditional diviner-healer on Monday when faced with a mysterious illness.

The prophet-healing churches, on the other hand, accept Christianity and look to the Bible for their spiritual authority. But they also accept the traditional world view in many respects. They believe in the reality of witchcraft and sorcery. Unlike the mission churches, they provide a Christian source of protection against these evil powers in prayer and the use of holy water because they believe that Jesus Christ has the power to protect and heal. They also believe that the Christian God reveals the future and the causes of misfortune through visions. Thus since the prophet-healing churches offer a substitute for the services of traditional diviner-healers, these churches are able to strictly forbid their members to consult with these practitioners, something that would be very difficult for the mission churches to enforce.

THE ALADURA: A DESCRIPTION

The Yoruba versions of these prophet-healing churches are called Aladura churches. The word *Aladura* means "owner-of-prayer" or "praying man," and comes from the fact that the prophets are noted for their loud, powerful prayers. Most Yoruba are either Christian or Muslim, but the Aladura churches are quite widespread and seem to be growing in strength.

A visitor in one of the larger Yoruba towns in western Nigeria today would first be struck by the visibility of both Islam and Christianity. Although Christians do not affect a distinctive dress, Muslims do, and their turbans and robes are much in evidence in the marketplace or along the streets. Purdah, the custom of secluding women from public observation, is a rarity among Yoruba Muslims; but the occasional veiled woman provides a startling sight in contrast with the ordinary, hardworking, nonveiled Yoruba woman. Christians, however, display their presence and power by the numerous signs proclaiming this C.M.S. (Church Missionary Society, Anglican) primary school or that Methodist secondary school or someone else's teacher-training college. Muslim educational facilities of the modern sort exist but are far fewer in number, although the visitor who wanders from the main thoroughfares might encounter a mallam, or Muslim clergyman, teaching his pupils the Koran on the front porch of his house.

Most conspicuous of all, of course, are the places of worship erected by the different religions. The town's central mosque will most likely be a large and impressive structure matched only by the church or cathedral of the Anglicans, although, depending upon the town, the largest Methodist or Baptist church may rival, or even surpass, that of the Anglicans and Muslims. Lesser places of worship for all faiths abound. In contrast, traditional Yoruba religion has neither schools, distinctive garments, nor, with very few exceptions, places of worship of sufficient size to attract the attention of the uninitiated visitor. But although traditional African religion is almost as invisible as the breeze, through the persistence of the primal world view, it is just about as pervasive.

The buildings for the Aladura churches are usually (but not always) poor imitations of the mission churches. The names, however, are different and striking: Cherubim and Seraphim Society, The Church of the Lord, The Christ Apostolic Church, The Regeneration Church of Christ, The Light of Jesus Church, and so on. Of even greater interest are the actions and dress of some of these groups. If a visitor is fortunate enough to find a Cherubim and Seraphim prophet conducting an open-air preaching service, he or she will most likely see a display of religious virtuosity in music, prayer dance, and preaching that will stir the non-Yoruba soul even though the person might not understand a word of it.

The prophet will be garbed in his prayer gown—a white or sometimes more adventurously colored robe, cut like an Anglican cassock. Shouting and gesturing his message in a rhythmic cadence to the circle of casual onlookers, he will suddenly break into song, perhaps accompanying himself with a hand bell (the kind once used in schools to summon children, but never with this effect). A powerful beat is maintained and a dance step is taken up. The song is a simple lyric whose Yoruba intonations match the music, thus doubly impressing its meaning deep into the listeners who themselves might dance a few steps or join in the chorus. Then he will return to his harangue which will be followed by a prayer in which God is addressed with vigor, directness, and almost hypnotic repetitiveness. The prayer elicits choruses of responses by the onlookers as they share in the petitions for God's help against witchcraft, his victory over sin, his guidance over their lives that they may not meet with any sickness or misfortune, his support in their battles with those who would wish them harm, and his blessing for their or, if male, their wives' wish to become pregnant and deliver a healthy child.

If the visitor follows the prophet back to his church, or if he or she visits any of the other Aladura churches which are bound to be numerous but, owing to their small size and relative poverty, rather unobtrusive in the urban landscape, the visitor will be welcomed with warm Yoruba hospitality. Depending upon the Aladura denomination the visitor may be requested politely to remove his or her shoes before entering the sanctuary, as the interior is deemed holy. In such a church of the Cherubim and Seraphim type, despite the fact that it is not yet time for one of the frequent daily services, there may be people in the church—some lying on mats on the floor, others sitting on plain wooden benches. Inquiry reveals that they are sick people who are living in the sanctuary in order to absorb its holiness and its power, which is believed to have healing properties. Also believed to heal is the holy water, encased in bottles which formerly may have held Sprite or Squash or even Silver Top gin, but which now cluster, labelless, on the floor near the altar or on a special table set aside for this purpose.

The aura of shabby sanctity conveyed by the interior is no different from the prophet's appearance at this time when a service is not in progress. His robe may be slightly tattered and in need of a washing. His manner has little in it of sanctimoniousness, of hushed expectancy in the presence of divinity. The attitude toward him of the afflicted, who are reclining in the sanctuary, suggests neither reverence nor awe, but simply the appropriate Yoruba tone of respect to someone higher in status than they. This is not especially remarkable because, while his worldly attainments and lineage may be relatively slight (his education is rarely above the level of primary school), those of his clients who attempt a cure in this fashion are usually lower still in status.

A client asks the prophet to pray for him. Without even the smallest barrier or reverent silence between the profane and the sacred, the prophet shuts his eyes, places his hand on the person's head, and immediately launches into a shouting, pleading, yet increasingly powerful prayer directed toward his request for God's help. Some Aladura prophets possess a greater facility than others for eliciting a feeling of God's power and holiness through their prayers, but the visitor who observes several prophets can well understand why the Yoruba call these churches "Aladura."

The Sunday service is only one of a number of services the church holds during the week. Every morning, early, the day begins with prayer and singing; every workday is brought to a close the same way and there may be several services in between. Shorter than the two- or three-hour Sunday service, the services during the week do not have a sermon and attract fewer attendants. One or more mornings during the week the prophet will have "clinic" services which are especially dedicated to healing. The women who attend this service arrive with their bottles, pails, or even buckets of water which will be blessed at the conclusion of the service. Some of them are regulars at one of the mission churches on Sunday, making their relationship with the Aladura church a part-time one.

Some Aladura churches have weekly "watch-night" services. These occur on Saturday beginning late in the evening and continuing until the Holy Spirit, who is summoned to possess the faithful, leaves the participants sweating, exhausted, but joyful with the confidence that God has spoken directly to them through the revelations given by the babblings of the twitching, eye-rolling, limb-jerking, possessed humans chosen by him that evening as his vessels. Adding to their joy is their confidence that witches have been directly confronted during their hours of terrible activity by the power of the living God and his son, Jesus, and vanquished from their lives, no more to cause sickness, misfortune, and death.

Periodically, the enthusiasm of the watch-night service is reconstituted during a series of weekly early evening services called revivals, which are meant to stir the hearts of the faithful and to exhibit the power of God to those questing and afflicted individuals who are not members of the congregation.

ALADURA CHURCHES
COMPARED WITH MISSION CHURCHES

Investigating further this religious phenomenon of the Aladura, the visitor begins to perceive that the various Aladura congregations reveal some discernible regularities despite their apparent diversity. First, almost all of the Aladura churches both claim to be Christian and are Christian in the objective sense of interpreting divinity in orthodox Christian trinitarian terms, strongly rejecting the traditional Yoruba deities and associated cults and practitioners, and relying upon the Bible as the ultimate source of spiritual authority.

Secondly, Aladura churches share distinctive emphases which differentiate them from the mission churches. The Aladuras are more enthusiastic in their worship; they incorporate more taboos in their beliefs about correct conduct; their interpretations of the Bible are augmented by direct revelations through dreams, visions, and possession; and their leadership includes prophets whose healing and divinatory activities (by means of visions) are one of the most important activities. The essential thrust of Aladura church life is toward this-worldly salvation from those ever-present threats to their members: magic, witchcraft, and the work of spirits. This is accomplished by the religious power conveyed through the prophet and the church.

ISLAM AND THE PRIMAL WORLD VIEW

Groups similar to the prophet-healing churches have not appeared among African Muslims. The reason for this lies in the initial acceptance of the traditional world view by Muslims who seek to spread their religion to traditionalists. At first Islam's demands on the new convert are minimal. For example, although a fundamental break with the traditional religion is demanded, consultation with diviner-healers is generally tolerated. The new believers can also consult with Muslim diviner-healers who may, for example, make charms which contain appropriate verses of the Koran. Over time, through the process which scholars have called Islamization, African Islam becomes progressively more orthodox and intolerant of traditional magic. This process generally takes many decades, however.

THE IMPORTANCE OF
THE AFRICAN PRIMAL RELIGIONS

Why study the primal religions if they are rapidly declining? The answer should now be clear. First, they are still practiced as religions by millions of Africans. Second, the primal world view continues to be a living force in changing African society. It affects the minds and actions of virtually every African today, no matter what his or her present religious belief. It has fused with Christianity in the prophet-healing churches, one of which—the large Kimbanguist Church of Zaire—has even been accepted into the membership of the World Council of Churches. There are also signs that African Christian theologians are developing an "African theology" which will reflect some of the religious insights of the primal world view and put them in a Christian context. In this way the primal religions will continue to be important for a long time to come.

African primal religions are also important for a final reason, however. Their world view has something to teach us. Today, changes in Western society have gone so far that a concern for groups, respect for older people, and a oneness with nature (to take three themes from African primal culture) are all too often overbalanced by an excessive individualism, the cult of youth, and an exploitative attitude toward nature. Often Western religions become too detached from the everyday concerns of life that affect each of us. African primal religions, on the other hand, echo these universal human concerns and offer a fresh, humanistic perspective on these matters. Traditional Africans, after all, share our common humanity. Consider, in this regard, this Yoruba poem on love which is part of the poetry of the Egungun masqueraders:

> We only know the one we love
> Not the one who loves us.
> Love is of many kinds.
> One love says: if you die let me die with you.
> Another love says: if you buy the stew, I will buy the rice.
> There is love of the eye,
> There is love of the mouth.
> The love of the wife is different,
> The love of the husband is different,
> The love of the father is different,

The love of the mother is greatest.
It is love that makes the goat share her husband's beard.
"I see the one I want to marry."
The father says: "Don't you know that his father is deaf?"
"If the whip howls on my back, and thunder shouts in heaven,
    If you tie me to the pillar and feed me with grass like a horse,
    I will still know whom I love!"

Minaret of an Islamic mosque in Ibadan, Nigeria.

Notes

Chapter 1: Introduction
1. E. B. Idowu, *Olodumare: God in Yoruba Belief* (Harlow, Essex, England: Longman Group Ltd., 1966) p. 141.

2. Ibid.

3. Ibid., p. 143.

Chapter 2: Many But One
1. This map is adapted from George Peter Murdock's tribal map of Africa in his book *Africa: Its People and Their Culture* (New York: McGraw-Hill, 1959).

2. Robin Horton, "African Traditional Thought and Western Science," *Africa*, Vol. 31 (1967), pp. 50–71, 155–87.

Chapter 3: Gods, Divinities, Ancestors, and Spirits
1. Gunter Wagner, "The Abaluyia of Kavirondo (Kenya)" in Daryll Forde, ed., *African Worlds* (New York: Oxford University Press, 1954), pp. 37–38.

2. E. E. Evans-Pritchard, *Nuer Religion* (New York: Oxford University Press, 1965.) E. B. Idowu, *Olodumare: God In Yoruba Belief* (Harlow, Essex, England: Longman Group Ltd., 1966).

3. John V. Taylor, *The Primal Vision* (London: SCM Press, 1963), p. 77.

4. Ibid., p. 156.

5. E. B. Idowu, *African Traditional Religion: A Definition* (Maryknoll, N. Y.: Orbis Press, 1973), p. 184.

6. Kenneth Little, "The Mende in Sierra Leone" in Daryll Forde, ed., *African Worlds* (New York: Oxford University Press, 1954), pp. 123–24.

Chapter 4: Festivals, Rites of Passage, and Diviner-Healers
1. Robin Horton, *The Gods as Guests: An Aspect of Kalabari Religious Life* (Lagos, Nigeria: Nigeria Magazine Special Publication, 1960).

2. Ibid., pp. 34, 35.

3. Noel Q. King, *Religions of Africa* (New York: Harper & Row, 1970), pp. 63–64.

4. This translation is from the collection of Yoruba odus which an American anthropologist, William Bascom, published. *Ifa Divination: Communication Between Gods and Men in West Africa* (Bloomington, Ind.: Indiana University Press, 1969), pp. 203–4.

Chapter 5: The Nature and Destiny of Humanity
1. Taylor, *Primal Vision,* pp. 56–66.

2. John Middleton, *Lugba Religion* (Oxford, Eng.: Clarendon Press, 1960), p. 31.

3. Taylor, *Primal Vision,* p. 93.

4. John S. Mbiti, *African Religions and Philosophy* (New York: Praeger, 1969), p. 176.

Chapter 6: Forces
1. Placide Tempels, *Bantu Philosophy* (New York: Oxford Univ. Press, 1959), p. 40.

2. Taylor, *Primal Vision,* p. 75.

3. Chinua Achebe, *Things Fall Apart* (New York: Fawcett World Library, 1969), p. 26.

Chapter 7: Evil

1. Mary Douglas, *The Lele of Kasai* (New York: Oxford Univ. Press, 1963), p. 261.

2. William Simmons, *Eyes of the Night: Witchcraft Among a Senegalese People* (Boston: Little, Brown and Co., 1971).

3. Ibid., p. 108.

Chapter 8: Dying But Very Much Alive

1. Donald G. Morrison, Robert C. Mitchell, et al., *Black Africa: A Comparative Handbook*, 2nd ed. (New York: Free Press, forthcoming).

Chapter 9: Prophet-Healing Religion

1. Ibid.

Suggested Readings

Achebe, Chinua. *Things Fall Apart*. New York: Fawcett World Library, Crest Book, 1969. Excellent novel by a leading Nigerian novelist. It describes the role of religion in an Ibo village before and after the arrival of the British.

Bowen, Elenor S. *Return to Laughter*. New York: Natural History Press, 1964. A novelistic account of an American anthropologist's experiences among the Tiv people in central Nigeria. Bowen is the pen name of Laura Bohannan. This fascinating novel portrays role of magic and witchcraft very well.

Idowu, E. Bolaji. *Olodumare: God in Yoruba Belief*. New York: Longman, 1966. Well-written description of Yoruba religion by a Yoruba professor of religion at Ibadan University.

King, Noel Q. *Religions of Africa*. New York: Harper & Row, 1970. Good analysis of African religions with detailed descriptions of the beliefs and practices of individual tribes. This book also contains an excellent long bibliographic essay.

Mair, Lucy. *Witchcraft*. New York: McGraw-Hill, 1969. Well-written paperback with many illustrations. Mair is a well-known English anthropologist. Her book considers witchcraft all over the world, but many of the peoples discussed are African.

Simmons, William S. *Eyes of the Night: Witchcraft Among a Senegalese People*. Boston: Little, Brown & Co., 1971. Although this book focuses on witchcraft, this short and well-written paperback also provides a good account of the general way of life of the Badyaranke.

Trimingham, J. Spencer. *Influence of Islam Upon Africa*. New York: Praeger Publishers, 1968. Short but profound analysis of the role of Islam in Africa by a leading scholar of Islam.

Glossary

Aladura churches. The Yoruba form of the prophet-healing churches.

ancestral cult. A set of religious practices directed toward the dead forebearers of a family.

animism. Belief in spirits; in particular the attribution of an innate soul to natural phenomena or objects.

Arabian Peninsula. The territory across the Red Sea from Africa which contains Mecca and Medina, the two Muslim religious centers where Muhammad founded the religion in the seventh century.

Berbers. Indigenous, non-Arab peoples who live in North Africa and who were the bridge between North Africa and black Africa in promoting the spread of Islam.

communal religion. A religion practiced by a particular human community such as a village, a kingdom, or a tribe.

creation myth. A traditional story which explains the origins of the world and of human beings. In African primal societies the creation myth is passed down from generation to generation by the oral tradition.

cult. A set of religious practices which are typically practiced by a group of people.

the Dead. Among the Kalabari of Nigeria, the Dead are the spirits of human beings. The Kalabari believe these spirits escape from their bodies at death and continue to exist in the supernatural world in a society which is similar to that of the living Kalabari.

divination. The art of interpreting supernatural causation and future events.

diviner. Someone who practices the art of interpreting supernatural causation and future events.

diviner-healer. Someone who practices the art of divination and who also administers herbal medicine or in other ways treats the sick.

divinities. A set of spiritual powers which rule over some area of the world or some special activity in human life. In everyday language they are "lesser gods."

Dominicans. A Roman Catholic religious order.

East Africa. Consists primarily of Kenya, Uganda, and Tanzania, although Rwanda, Burundi, Somalia, Ethiopia, Sudan, Malawi, Zambia, and Mozambique may also be placed in this geographic region.

Egungun Society. A religious secret society among the Yoruba. The Egungun masqueraders represent the spirits of the ancestors, and the society's annual festival is held to commemorate the ancestral spirits. Membership is restricted to men.

forces. Spiritual powers which affect human life.

initiation rites. Religious rituals which mark the rite of passage from the status of youth to the status of adult in African traditional societies.

institutional religion. A religion which is formally embodied in a social structure of religious specialists, cults, rituals, and festivals.

Islam. A religion based on the teachings of the Prophet Muhammad; also called the Muslim religion.

Jesuits. A Roman Catholic religious order.

Kongo. An African people whose territory spreads across the three contemporary nations of Zaire, Angola, and the Congo. In the sixteenth century the Kongo Kingdom established diplomatic and trading relations with Portugal.

life's destiny. The path of life which an individual is given at the moment of creation by the Supreme Being. Although the individual has no memory of his or her destiny, it is believed to determine his or her fortunes throughout life unless it is altered through religious means.

living-dead. A term, coined by John Mbiti, which refers to the persistence of a person's individual-soul for some time after death.

mission churches. The churches founded by Western Christian missionaries such as the Anglican, Methodist, Baptist, and Seventh-Day Adventist churches.

Muhammad (A.D. 570–632). Prophet and founder of Islam.

multiple self. The view of the human personality as consisting of a set of distinct entities. Typically these entities are the life-soul, the individual-soul or personality-soul, the ancestor-soul, and the transcendent-soul.

Muslim. An individual adherent to the Islamic religion.

Nirvana. The Buddhist state of absolute blessedness in which the individual is finally released from the cycle of reincarnations.

North Africa. The five countries lying north of the Sahara: Morocco, Algeria, Tunisia, Libya, and the Arab Republic of Egypt.

oracle. A priest who serves a deity which has the power to see the future and to discern the spiritual meaning of the present.

oral tradition. The method of transmitting history and religious traditions from one generation to another by spoken rather than written means. In primal societies, religious and historical specialists memorize these traditions with great accuracy.

ori. The Yoruba word for head and also for the transcendent-soul of the individual.

Oro Society. A male religious secret society among the Yoruba. The society's activities are not supposed to be observed by women under any circumstances. The society is believed to have power over witches and functions to protect the people from witchcraft.

peasants. People who live in a society which is at the peasant level of social organization. This level is characterized by literacy, cities, universal religions, and individual land ownership.

polygamy. Practice of having more than one spouse at a time. In Africa the form of polygamy that is practiced is polygyny—one husband and more than one wife.

primal religion. The word *primal* connotes something basic, fundamental, prior. Primal religions are the nonuniversal religions of the world's preliterate peoples.

primal world view. The assumptions about the nature of the world, the nature and destiny of human beings, and the nature of good and evil which are embodied in the primal religions.

prophet-healing churches. A type of African Christian church which evolved out of the interaction between mission Christianity and the African world view. These churches emphasize the use of Christian religious power to help the believer achieve his or her life's destiny in this life.

reincarnation. The condition of being reborn in another body. In African primal religions, it is believed that the transcendent-soul of a recently deceased ancestor might be reincarnated in an infant born to a member of the family. This "partial" reincarnation is different from the Hindu and Buddhist "total" reincarnation, in which an individual's total spiritual self is reborn.

rites of passage. Religious rituals which are performed at turning points in an individual's life, such as birth, marriage, and death.

Sahel region. A geographic region of low rainfall located in the interior of West Africa on the border of the Sahara. It extends from Mauritania to Sudan.

shade. The spirit of a particular dead person which persists for some time after death.

sorcerer. An antisocial practitioner who causes evil by manipulating material objects and performing rituals.

South Africa. A large country at the southern tip of Africa. The country's white inhabitants first arrived in the seventeenth century; and, although outnumbered four to one by the nonwhites, they have continued to retain control of the country by the controversial policy of apartheid, or racial separation.

spirit. A supernatural being.

Sufi. A type of Muslim mystical society or brotherhood which is organized around a primary Muslim saint and which believes in the powers of direct revelation from Allah through the training of body, mind, and spirit.

Supreme Being. The transcendent, all-powerful creator deity which exists in the background above all the other spirits and divinities.

taboo. A prohibition excluding something from use because of its sacred nature.

tribe. A people who share a common way of life or culture and a sense of identity. Typically the culture has a relatively simple technology.

tribesmen. People who live in a society which is at the tribal level of social organization. This level is characterized by oral traditions, small towns or villages, local religions, and land ownership that is vested in the community.

unilineal descent. The cultural rule of tracing one's descent through only one parent. Matrilineal descent (through the mother) and patrilineal descent (through the father) are both common in black Africa.

Village Heroes. Among the Kalabari of Nigeria, the Village Heroes are spiritual beings who are believed to have once lived in the village and who eventually tired of living on earth and vanished.

Water People. Among the Kalabari of Nigeria, the Water People are supernatural beings who are believed to control aspects of the aquatic environment of this fishing people, such as the water level and the movements of the fish.

West Africa. Area stretching from north of the mouth of the Senegal River to Lake Chad. It includes Mauritania, Senegal, Gambia, Guinea, Guinea-Bissau, Sierra Leone, Ivory Coast, Ghana, Togo, Benin, and Nigeria along the West African coast and, in the interior, Mali, Niger, Upper Volta, and Chad.

witch. An antisocial person who is able to harm others by an innate spiritual power.

witch doctor. A term used by Westerners to refer to diviner-healers. As the British expert on primal religions, Harold W. Turner, has pointed out, the term is misleading, because these practitioners have nothing to do with witches except to fight them and to protect their clients from them.

Yoruba tribe. An African people living in southwestern Nigeria. Numbering more than ten million, they are one of the largest of Nigeria's peoples.